CELTIC COOKBOOK

Traditional Recipes From the Six Celtic Nations

Helen Smith-Twiddy

HIPPOCRENE BOOKS

New York

Originally published in Wales by Y Lolfa Cyf.

Hippocrene edition, 1998.

For information, address:
Hippocrene Books, Inc.
171 Madison Avenue
New York, NY 10016

Library of Congress Cataloging-in-Publication Data

Smith-Twiddy, Helen.
    Celtic cookbook : traditional recipes from the six Celtic lands /
    Helen Smith-Twiddy — Hippocrene hbk. ed.
        p. cm.
    Includes index.
    ISBN 0-7818-0579-1
    1. Cookery, Celtic.   I. Title.
TX717.2S64   1998
641.59'2916—dc21   97-42823
                                                                CIP

Printed in the United States of America.

CORNISH

Chowder

4 tablespoons butter
2 small onions (chopped)
4 slices bacon (chopped)
1 cup diced carrots
1 pound fresh peas (cooked)
2 cups diced potatoes
1 cup chopped celery
4 cups white sauce
salt and pepper
1 pound cooked shellfish

Heat the butter in a large pan. Fry the onions and bacon lightly. Add the chopped and diced vegetables. Add the white sauce and seasonings. Add the fish. Simmer for about 15 minutes. Serve with Dorset Knobs. (Recipe in Bread and Cake section)
Makes 4 servings.

Shrimp Soup

2 tablespoons butter
1¼ cup cooked prawns
2 cups water
salt and pepper
3 cups fresh milk
2 cups potato soup
2 small onions, chopped
parsley
dash of paprika

Melt butter in a large pan. Add prawns and cook slightly (until warmed through). Add the water, salt and pepper, butter, milk, and potato soup. Bring just to the boil but do not boil. Keep just at simmering point for 10 minutes. Chill and serve with chopped onions and parsley on the top. Dust with paprika.

Makes 6 servings.

Lobster Soup

1 large of each: carrot, onion, potato and four sticks of celery (all
   chopped)
1 tablespoon butter
some flour (to coat)
1 pound raw lobster meat (cubed)
salt and pepper
2 cups rice
2 cups fish stock
1 cup dry white wine
dash of brandy
some light cream

Sauté chopped vegetables in butter. Dust some flour over the vegetables as they cook. Add the lobster meat. Season with salt and pepper to taste. Add rice, stock, and wine. Cook for about 1 hour. Purée in a blender. Return to pan, re-heat, add brandy, serve and add a dash of cream in each bowl.

Makes 4 servings.

Pea Pods Soup

1 pound pea pods
2 medium sized potatoes, chopped
2 medium sized onions, chopped
1 tablespoon butter
pinch of flour
salt and pepper
3 cups stock

Chop up pea pods roughly, add potatoes and onions. Fry in the butter, add some flour to thicken slightly. Season with salt and pepper

CONTENTS

Soups

BRETON

Consomme

4 cups beef stock
Vegetables: selection of carrots, onions, cauliflower and turnips
    (chopped)
½ lb. stewing beef, cubed
salt and pepper
3 tablespoons sweet sherry

Make sure there is no fat on the stock. Cut up meat and vegetables into small pieces. Place in a large saucepan. Season with salt and pepper to taste. Cook until the meat is tender. Strain through a clean cloth or sieve. Add the sherry just before serving. Sprinkle some chopped parsley on top prior to serving.
    Makes 4 servings.

St. Brieuc Vegetable Soup

16 cups meat stock
salt and pepper
4 large tomatoes, peeled
2 pounds green beans
6 large potatoes
½ cup pasta sheets
3 cups grated Swiss cheese, divided

In a very large pan place the stock and salt and pepper to taste. Bring to a boil slowly. Chop up the tomatoes: clean and string beans. Peel potatoes and cut up into small pieces. Break pasta sheets into manageable pieces. Add the vegetables and pasta to the stock and cook slowly until vegetables are cooked. Before serving add half the cheese—do not boil once the cheese has been added. Put remainder of cheese in a bowl and serve with the soup at the table.
Makes 6 servings.

Pot au Feu

1 pound stewing beef (preferably shin)
4 cups cold water
1 each: leek, carrot, turnip, rutabaga, stick of celery, cabbage,
     large potato
Bouquet garni
a pinch of nutmeg
a few cloves
a pinch of peppercorn
½ cup rice

Tie the meat to keep its shape. Place in a large stewpot with the water. Simmer slowly for an hour. Peel, wash and cut up the vegetables into small pieces. Add to the meat. Add seasonings and cook for another hour. About ¼ hour before the end of the cooking time, add the rice. Serve very hot with fresh crusty bread.

If this soup is not all finished at one serving, more vegetables can be added as needed and cooked again. A Pot au Feu is always cooking in most kitchens in France.

Makes 4 servings.

Onion Soup

2 pounds onions
5 tablespoons butter
¼ cup flour
salt and pepper
8 cups beef stock
¾ cup grated strong Parmesan cheese
½ cup port or sherry
1 cup grated Swiss cheese

Cut onions into rings. Melt butter in a large pan and add onions. Cook until transparent. Sprinkle the flour over the onions and allow the flour to be absorbed. Add the salt and pepper to taste and stock. Cook slowly until the onions are tender. Add the Parmesan cheese and

cook another 15 minutes or so. Before serving add port or sherry and bring back to the boil. Add the Swiss cheese and serve with croutons.
    Makes 6 servings.

Fish Soup

½ lb. sardines
4 medium sized mackerel
6 small scad*
1 clove garlic
2 shallots, chopped
4 onions, chopped (divided)
8 cups water
1 potato per person
bread (2 or 3 days old)
salt, pepper, fresh butter

*not easily obtainable outside Brittany; however, mullet or gurnard would be excellent substitutes.

Clean the fish, but retain the heads. Remove scales. Dry fish thoroughly. Boil the garlic, ¾ of the chopped onions, shallots, salt and pepper in the water for 5 minutes. Now add the potatoes, whole. When potatoes are almost cooked, add all the fish together and increase heat to bring to a boil once again. Allow to boil for five minutes and reduce heat. Place a generous portion of fresh butter in a pan and heat; add remaining chopped onion and sauté; in the meantime add very thin pieces of bread to the soup. Allow soup to stand. If you so wish, strain before serving as perhaps the garlic will have caused the onions to turn a bluish color. Add the fried onion to the surface of the soup. Serve very hot.
    Makes 4 servings.

to taste. Add stock. Cook until vegetables are soft. Purée in blender to make smooth. Chill and serve cold.

Makes 4 servings.

Watercress Soup

1 pound potatoes
1 bunch shallots
3 bunches watercress
¼ cup flour
1 tablespoon butter
3 cups white stock
salt and pepper
some cream

Peel and chop potatoes. Chop shallots, tear watercress into stems. Sprinkle flour on vegetables and fry slightly in butter. Add stock, cook for about 1 hour. Season with salt and pepper to taste. Purée mixture in a blender. Serve hot with swirls of cream.

Makes 4 servings.

MANX

Manx Broth

1 pound beef shin
1 pound mixed chopped vegetables (potatoes, carrots, turnips
    and onions)
salt and black pepper
½ cup barley

Place the piece of meat into a large soup pan and cover with cold water. Simmer gently until the meat is cooked. Take out and put on a platter, reserving the stock. (The meat can be used cold for another meal). Add the diced vegetables and season with salt and pepper to taste. Simmer gently for 1 hour. About 10 minutes before serving this soup, drop in small parsley dumplings and cook in the broth. Make as follows:

2 tablespoons butter
¾ cup all-purpose flour
2 tablespoons chopped parsley
few drops water

Rub butter into flour. Add parsley. Make into a soft dough. Form into small balls.

This is a dish that is still served on the Island when the wedding feast is a sit down one.

Makes 4 servings.

Fish Soup

½ pound smoked fish (uncooked)
½ pound white fish
2 tablespoons butter
¼ cup flour
2 cups white stock
2 large onions, chopped
1 cup milk
salt and pepper
cream to garnish
parsley to garnish
1 prawn per person (to garnish)

Remove all bones from fish. Flake. Melt butter, toss fish into butter, coat with flour. Fry lightly until slightly browned. Add stock, onions, milk, and salt and pepper to taste. Simmer until fish is cooked. Remove and purée in a blender. Re-heat and add cream, parsley, and a cooked prawn to each soup bowl.

Makes 4 servings.

Carrot and Parsnip Soup

butter to fry vegetables
½ lb. carrots (chopped)
½ lb. parsnips (chopped)
1 medium onion, chopped
flour to coat vegetables
salt and pepper
4 cups stock (½ milk, ½ stock)
few ounces of single cream
2 oz. mild cheddar cheese
pinch of nutmeg

Melt butter, add chopped carrots, parsnips, and onions. Coat with flour. Add salt and pepper to taste. Cook for a few minutes until lightly browned. Add stock. Simmer for an hour or so. Remove from stove and purée mixture in food processor of blender. Return to stove and reheat.

Before serving swirl some cream on top and add a pinch of mild grated cheese and a small amount of nutmeg.

Makes 4 servings.

Vegetable Soup

This soup would be made from what was available in the garden, both grown vegetables and vegetation like nettles and wild watercress.

few rinds or small scraps of bacon
¼ cup each chopped and washed nettles (tops only as they are sweeter), watercress, spring onions, carrots, potatoes, rutabaga.
1 tablespoon of flour to thicken
salt and pepper
2 cups stock (more if too thick)

Fry the bacon, add the vegetables, toss in the flour and salt and pepper, brown lightly. Add stock. Simmer for about 1 hour. Purée in a blender. Serve hot.

Makes 4 to 6 servings.

Ham Broth

A shank of uncooked ham with quite a bit of meat still on it
4 cups water
2 oz pearl barley
2 small potatoes
2 small onions
2 small carrots
¼ rutabaga
(all vegetables finely chopped)
salt and pepper

Boil ham in water stock for about 1½ hour. Skim the top. Add the barley, vegetables and salt and pepper and simmer for another hour. Serve hot with warm bread.

Makes 4 servings.

IRISH

Potato Soup

2 sticks butter
3 lbs. old potatoes, peeled and chopped
6 large leeks, chopped
salt and pepper
12 cups good brown stock
1 cup thin cream or top of the milk

Melt the butter in a large stew pot. Add the chopped up potatoes and the leeks (chopped up into small pieces). Cook until tender. Season with salt and pepper to taste. Add the stock and cook for 2 hours. Before serving add the cream.

Makes 6 to 8 servings.

Ham and Pea Soup

4 medium onions
4 large potatoes
1 stick butter
1 lb. piece of boiling ham
salt and pepper
½ lb. diced peas
5 cups white stock
¼ cup flour
pinch of parsley

Wash and cut up the onions and potatoes. Melt butter. Add the onions and potatoes and the meat chopped up into small pieces. Brown slightly. Season with salt and pepper. Add the soaked peas and stock. Simmer for 2 hours, on a low heat. Thicken with the flour if necessary before serving. Sprinkle with parsley.

Makes 4 servings.

Fish Soup

2 lbs. assorted shell fish (cockles, clams, mussels and some
    white fish)
2 small potatoes, peeled and diced
2 small onions, diced
salt and pepper
3 pints of fish stock
3 tablespoons cream
pinch of parsley

Remove the fish from the shells. Add the diced potatoes and onions to the shell fish and season with salt and pepper. Pour the stock over. Simmer until the vegetables and fish are cooked and before serving add the cream. Sprinkle parsley over the top. Do not boil once the cream has been added as the soup will curdle.

Makes 4 to 6 servings.

Creamed Parsnip and Apple Soup

1 lb. parsnips, chopped
1 lb. apples (tart ones), chopped
2 large onions, chopped
flour to coat
butter
pinch black pepper
salt
4 cups beef stock

Put all vegetables into a large pan. Coat with flour. Fry lightly in the butter. Add pepper and salt. Add stock and cook for about 1 hour. Purée in blender and serve hot with Soda Bread.

Makes 4 servings.

Oxtail Soup

butter
1 lb. cut oxtails (meat only)
1 each: potato, carrot, onion (all chopped)
1 stalk celery, chopped
flour (to fry and coat meats)
salt and pepper
4 cups stock
1 cup sherry
1 tablespoon tomato paste
1 cup milk

Melt butter, coat oxtails and chopped vegetables with flour and salt and pepper. Cook for about 5 minutes. Pour over stock and sherry. Bring to the boil and simmer for 2 hours. Purée and return to pan. Add tomato paste, add milk and cook for a further 30 minutes, simmering slowly. Serve with warm soda bread.

Makes 6 servings.

SCOTLAND

Cock a Leekie

1 boiling fowl
8 cups stock
1 bunch leeks, diced
1 lb. onions (white), diced
salt and pepper

Put the fowl in a large pot. Cover with the stock and diced vegetables. Season with salt and pepper to taste. Simmer for 3 - 4 hours. Cool. Skim the fat from the top. Re-heat to serve and serve very hot with fresh bread.
Makes 6 servings.

Powsowdie

1 sheep's head
1 mutton flank
approx. 8 cups water
6 large carrots
6 large onions
4 small turnips
4 small potatoes
1 leek
½ cup barley
½ cup dried peas
salt and pepper
parsley

Clean the head and place in water overnight. Clean out the eyes and remove the brain. Place the head and mutton in sufficient water to cover, and simmer for 1 hour. Cool and skim off fat. Peel and slice carrots, onions, turnips, potatoes, and leek and add to the broth. Add barley and dried peas. Season with salt and pepper to taste. Cook for a further 2 hours. Serve hot, sprinkled with parsley.

Makes 6 to 8 servings.

Partan Bree

1 large crab (boiled)
2 cups milk
½ cup rice
salt and pepper
3 cups white stock
Drop of anchovy essence
½ cup cream

Take the meat from the crab. Place milk and rice in a saucepan and bring to a boil. Simmer until rice is soft. Season with salt and pepper to taste. Add stock, crab meat, and essence. Stir until it boils. Stir in cream but do not boil after cream has been added. Serve hot.

Makes 4 to 6 servings.

Scotch Broth

4 oz. dried peas
1 neck of lamb
salt and pepper
4 oz. pearl barley
2 quarts water
½ cabbage
4 dried carrots
2 onions
1 leek
1 small turnip
parsley
4 small potatoes
parsley

Soak the peas overnight, or until soft. Discard the water. Place meat, salt and pepper, barley and the peas in a large pot. Simmer for 2 - 3 hours in water. Peel and chop the vegetables and add about one hour before serving. Serve hot, sprinkled with parsley.

Makes 6 to 8 servings.

Leek and Tattie Soup

1 lb. potatoes (chopped small)
3 small leeks (chopped)
2 tablespoons butter
¼ cup flour
2 cups stock
salt and pepper
4 ounces grated cheese

Chop the vegetables, fry gently in the butter. Coat with the flour. Add stock, season well with salt and pepper. Simmer for about an hour. Purée in a blender and return to pan. Reheat. Serve with a good pinch of mature cheese that will melt wonderfully in the hot soup.

Makes 4 servings.

WALES

Cawl Cennin

3 lbs. best end of neck
1 lb. leeks
2 onions
2 carrots
1 turnip
1 rutabaga
parsnips
8 potatoes
¼ cabbage
10 cups water
3 tablespoons chopped parsley
salt and pepper

Trim the fat from the meat. Peel and cut up the vegetables into small cubes. Cover with the water and add the parsley and salt and pepper. Cook for about 2 hours very slowly. Skim off any fat before serving. Serve as a main meal with fresh bread.

Traditionally cawl has to be eaten with a wooden spoon from a wooden bowl. This way there is no fear of burning mouth or fingers.

Makes 8 servings.

Pembroke Soup

6 cups good fish stock (made from fish heads etc.)
2 large onions, chopped
salt and pepper
pinch of cinnamon
½ stick butter
⅓ cup flour
36 shelled and prepared oysters

Simmer gently for about 3 to 4 hours the stock, onions, salt and pepper, and cinnamon. Melt the butter and stir in the flour. Thicken the stock with this. Sieve if there are any lumps. Put the oysters into a large soup bowl, pour the boiling soup over and serve with small brown rolls. (Recipe in Bread Section).
Makes 6 servings.

Cawl Afu

1 pig's liver
1 lb. onions
4 cups water
pepper
1 lb. potatoes, peeled and cubed
1 lb. carrots, rutabaga and parsnips (cut into small cubes)
salt

Cut up the liver and onions into small cubes. Gently simmer with the water for 2 hours. Add only the pepper at this stage as the salt toughens the liver. Half an hour before serving add the other vegetables. Cook gently and serve hot. The liver, after all the cooking, should have become almost like a purée. Season with salt before serving.
This soup was made when the farm pig met his doom. The bladder was blown up and used by the children as a football.
Makes 4 to 6 servings.

Cawl

2 lbs. best end of neck
2 lbs. potatoes
1 lb. leeks
1 lb. onions
1 lb. carrots, rutabaga or turnip
1 lb. bacon, cooked and diced
seasoning water

Trim meat and brown. Peel and cut vegetables into cubes. Place diced bacon and neck, plus seasoning into a crochan (a large Welsh stewpan) and cover with water. Simmer for 1 hour. Add vegetables and simmer for another hour. Serve hot with fresh bread.

Makes 6 servings.

Cream of Mussel Soup

Wash and clean very well about 1 lb. meat weight of mussels
Enough stock to cover (½ stock, ½ milk)
salt and pepper
¼ cup oatmeal to thicken

Cook mussels in a stewpot until the shells open. Strain the liquid and remove all the black parts and beards. Take out the mussels and discard all shells. Add to the liquid, season well with salt and pepper and add enough oatmeal to thicken soup. Reheat slowly.

Makes 4 servings.

Fish

BRETON

Sole Bonne Femme

½ cup shallots
½ cup sliced mushrooms
pinch chopped parsley
salt and pepper
2 lbs. sole fillets
1 cup dry white wine
1 cup cream
4 medium tomatoes, sliced

Use a wide bottomed pan for this dish as it will then be easier to cook the fish without breaking the fillets. Place the shallots, mushrooms, a sprinkle of the parsley and salt and pepper on the bottom of the pan. Put the fish on top and pour the wine over. Cover and simmer very gently for 5 minutes or until the fish flakes easily when prodded with a fork. Take out the fish when cooked and place on a platter and keep hot. Add the cream to the pan and boil until reduced by about a quarter. Be very careful not to cook too long, as sauce will burn easily. Pour over the fish and serve with more parsley and tomato slices. Serve with new boiled potatoes and a green salad.
Makes 4 servings.

Grilled Sardines

1 lb. fresh sardines (clean and remove backbone)
1 beaten egg
1 cup breadcrumbs
salt and pepper
oil to pour before grilling

Dip each fish in egg and then breadcrumbs. Season with salt and pepper. Place under a hot grill and drizzle over some oil. Grill until well browned on both sides.
Makes 4 servings.

Fish Terrine

½ lb. shrimps or prawns, cooked and shelled
½ lb. halibut, cooked and de-boned
½ stick butter
¼ cup chopped green shallots
½ teaspoon salt
¼ teaspoon fresh black pepper
¼ teaspoon tarragon
¼ teaspoon fresh chopped parsley
¼ cup plain flour
2 teaspoons white dry wine
2 teaspoons lemon juice
1¼ cups cream (top of milk will do)
2 well beaten eggs
cooked pink salmon (for garnish)

Blend the cooked fish (in separate batches) in an electric blender until quite smooth. Keep the white and pink fish separate. Melt the butter and fry the shallots until soft. Add the salt, pepper, tarragon, and parsley. Blend the flour with the wine and lemon juice into a smooth paste. Add to shallots, take from heat and add the cream. Add the beaten eggs and stir well. Mix enough of the sauce with the fish (still separate) to make into a runny mixture. Pour half the white fish mixture into a greased terrine (6-8 cup size) then add the pink fish, then the white. Chop up finely some pink salmon and place on top. This will sink into the sauce mixture a little and add color to the terrine. Cover the dish and stand in a large container of boiling water and bake for 30-40 minutes in a moderate (350 degree) oven. Remove and chill.

Serve with thin brown bread slices.
Makes 6 servings.

Creamed Halibut and Sorrell

½ stick butter
1 lb. halibut fillets
½ cup green shallots (chopped)
4 tablespoons dry white wine
2 tablespoons butter
¼ cup plain flour
salt and pepper
pinch cinnamon, nutmeg and some chopped parsley
1 cup good fish stock
1½ - 1¾ cups chopped sorrell
½ cup cream

In a pie dish, melt ½ stick of butter and arrange fish fillets on top. Sprinkle with shallots and the white wine. Cover and cook until the fish flakes. Melt the 2 tablespoons butter in a pan and add flour. Blend with the salt and pepper, cinnamon, nutmeg, and parsley until smooth. Add fish stock and cook. Add the chopped sorrell and cream and warm without boiling. Pour over the fish cutlets and serve at once.

Makes 4 servings.

Breton Whiting

1 lb. Whiting Fillets
1 tablespoon fresh mustard
1 small onion, chopped
salt and pepper
2 tablespoons butter
½ cup white wine
chopped parsley

Clean and dry the fish. Spread with mustard. Lay in a casserole dish. Sprinkle over the onion. Season well with salt and pepper. Dot with butter. Pour over the white wine and cover. Cook for about 45 minutes in a 350 degree oven (or until the fish is soft). Sprinkle the parsley over the top before serving.

Makes 4 servings.

CORNISH

Fish Gazy Pie

8 herrings or mackerel
3 uncooked potatoes, peeled
salt and pepper
few drops vinegar
4 eggs
½ cup cream
sufficient pastry to cover the top of a pie dish
parsley sprigs

Clean and bone the fish: leave the heads on. Grease a pie dish. Grate the potatoes and arrange to form a base. Place the fish on top with their heads towards the center. Season with the salt, pepper and vinegar. Beat the eggs and cream and pour over the fish. Lay the pastry on top and leave a hole in the center to allow the heads of the fish to poke out. Bake for 1 hour in moderate oven (350 degrees). Place a sprig of parsley on each fish head.

Makes 6 servings.

Singing Snails

12 snails
2 tablespoons butter
salt and pepper
some garlic

Drop snails into boiling water and boil for 30 minutes. Take off shells and cut away the hard meats. Put meat into a greased pie dish: cover with the butter pats and season with salt, pepper, and garlic. Cook for 10 minutes in hot oven (425 degrees). Serve with thin brown bread.

Makes 3 to 4 servings.

Potted Shrimps

1 stick butter
2 cups shrimps
2 tablespoons white wine or sweet cider
pinch nutmeg
salt and pepper
pinch garlic powder

Heat butter and add the prepared shrimps. Add wine and other ingredients. Heat gently but do not boil. Pot and eat cold with green salad.

Makes 4 to 6 servings.

Lampreys

These are rather similar to eels and according to some of the early monarchs of England were considered a great delicacy. The end product certainly tastes very much better than the raw product looks.

approx 2 lbs. lampreys
salt and pepper
juice of 1 lemon
1 cup dry white wine
1 small onion, chopped
pinch nutmeg

Clean and gut the fish. Place in a pie dish. Season well with salt and pepper, and lemon juice and pour over the wine. Add onion and nutmeg. Cook with the lid on for about 2 hours or until tender, in a slow oven (275-300 degrees).

Makes 4 to 6 servings.

Soused Herrings

6 Herring fillets
1 cup wine vinegar
1 cup water
pinch mace (crushed)
pinch of brown sugar
1 large onion (very finely chopped)

Place the fish fillets into a wide based casserole dish. Pour over the wine vinegar and water, add mace, sugar and the onion. Cover and cook for an hour in a moderately hot oven (375 degrees). Leave to cool in the liquids, when cold lift out and serve.

Makes 4 to 6 servings.

Jugged Kippers

Allow 1 kipper per person (filleted)
1 small glass port
Butter to dot over top before serving

Put the kippers into a fish kettle or large pan. Pour over a small amount of water and the port. Cook for 5 minutes. Drain and serve dotted with the butter.

MANX

Manx Kippers

2 kippers
2 tablespoons butter

Place the kippers on a shallow dish. Dot with butter and grill for about 3-4 minutes. Serve hot with thin brown bread.

Manx Herrings and Priddhas

Allow two herrings per person
Allow two medium potatoes per person
1 raw onion (sliced)

Scrub the potatoes and place in water to par boil. Lay the fish on top of the potatoes and cook fish. Drain potatoes and lift out fish carefully. Serve with raw onion rings and plenty of buttermilk to drink.

This is an old traditional Manx rhyme about this famous recipe:
>I'm a native of Peel
>And I think for a meal,
>That there's nothin' like priddhas and herrin'
>I was reared on the quay
>An' I followed the say
>An' its 'mighty good fishin' I'm gettin'.

The Tanrogans are the large scallops caught around the Island. The smaller ones are called Queenies. It is now much easier to purchase the Queenies from the local fishmongers.

Fish

Fried Herrings in Oatmeal

1 herring per person (filleted)
1 beaten egg
oatmeal to coat
oil to fry

Clean the herrings and dry well. Dip in the egg and then the oatmeal. Fry until golden brown on both sides. Serve with a wedge of lemon.

Creamed Crabbys

1 lb. mashed potatoes mixed with 2-3 ounces cream
¾ lb. cooked boned salmon
¼ lb. cooked boned white fish
2 oz. fine white breadcrumbs
salt and pepper
dash of tabasco sauce
pinch parsley (chopped)
1 beaten egg
oil to fry

Mix the potatoes and fish together until fine (no lumps). Add breadcrumbs, salt and pepper, tabasco sauce, parsley, and beaten egg. Mix well. Form into small cakes and cook in a shallow frypan until browned on both sides.
Makes 4 to 6 servings.

Queenies with a Cheese and Onion Sauce

10 queenies (sea scallops)
1 cup fish stock
2 small onions, chopped
salt and pepper

Sauce:

1 tablespoon butter
1 cup milk
1 tablespoon flour
4 oz. Cheddar cheese
1 onion, diced and cooked

Place the shelled Queenies in an ovenproof dish. Add stock and onion. Season with salt and pepper and bake in moderate oven (350 degrees) for about 15 minutes. Lift the scallops out of the dish and replace in their shells. Make the sauce by combining all ingredients and heating, and serve by pouring a little over each shell.

Makes 4 servings.

IRISH

Grilled Sole

½ stick butter
1 fillet of sole
1 beaten egg
brown breadcrumbs
1 cup small sliced mushrooms
salt and pepper

Melt butter in a flat frypan. Cup up sole fillet into fingers. Dip in butter, egg and breadcrumbs and cook in the butter till golden brown. Cook the sliced mushrooms in and around the sole fingers. Serve with a green salad. Season with salt and pepper to taste.
Makes 4 servings.

Irish Crab

lettuce
2 crabs (cooked)
½ cup fresh cream
1 cup mayonnaise
chopped parsley
salt and pepper
lemon juice

Arrange the lettuce in a salad bowl to form a base for the crab. Take out all the meat from the shells. Mix the cream and mayonnaise together. Add the parsley and season with the salt and pepper and lemon juice. Add crab meat. Pile the crab onto the lettuce leaves.
Shellfish is readily available in most parts of Ireland, but around the Dublin area shell fish is really not considered a delicacy, but simply one of the foods that the Emerald Isle provides for its people to eat and enjoy.
Makes 4 servings.

Scallops in a Cheese and Mushroom Sauce

8 - 10 medium-sized scallops
1 cup milk
½ stick butter
2 small onions, chopped
¼ cup flour
½ cup cream
4 dessert spoons sherry
salt and pepper
½ lb. button mushrooms, chopped and cooked
2 tablespoons breadcrumbs
4 oz. sharp cheese

Simmer the scallops in the milk until cooked. Keep the milk. Remove scallops from the shells and cut into thick slices. Melt the butter and add the chopped onion. Add flour and stir to ensure there are no lumps. Add the heated milk, cream and sherry. Season with salt and pepper. Add the cooked chopped mushrooms. Add sliced scallops, breadcrumbs, and cheese and mix well. Pile into scallop shells and cut a slice of butter to top each of the shells. Grill until the cheese browns.

Makes 4 servings.

Mussels in Butter

6 tablespoons butter
1 clove garlic (crushed)
some finely chopped parsley
12 mussels per person
¾ cup dry white wine

Soften the butter and mix with the crushed garlic and parsley. Chill for about an hour.

Clean the mussels and leave in cold water for an hour. Put the mussels into a large saucepan about ½ hour before the meal is to be served. Cook on a very high heat for about 5-6 minutes. Take out of the pan and arrange in separate dishes. Pour wine over mussels. Put a tablespoon of garlic butter over each mussel. Place under a hot grill and when the butter starts to sizzle, serve with thin brown bread.

Crab au Gratin

1 small onion
2 small tomatoes
2 small zucchini
2 tablespoons butter
½ lb. fresh crab meat
salt and pepper
1 oz. strong white cheese (grated)

Sauce:

2 tablespoons butter
¼ cup flour
½ cup milk
salt and pepper
dash of Irish Whiskey

Make a roux sauce with all the above ingredients except the whiskey. Add whiskey after the sauce is cooked, and do not reboil.

Chop the onion finely. Skin and slice the tomatoes. Slice the zucchini. Melt the butter in a heavy saucepan. Fry the zucchini and onions until soft. Arrange the zucchini in a buttered gratin dish, put the onions and tomatoes over the zucchini, put the crab meat on the top. Add the salt and pepper, pour over the sauce. Sprinkle the cheese over the dish. Place the dish in a hot oven (425 degrees) and cook for 15 to 20 minutes until the top is browned.

Makes 4 servings.

SCOTLAND

Creamed Haddie

1 lb. Haddock fillets
½ lb. fresh mushrooms
3 skinned tomatoes, sliced
1½ cups white sauce
2 oz. grated cheese
salt and pepper

Grease a pie dish. Cover the base with the fish fillets. Slice the mushrooms and sprinkle over the fish. Put the tomatoes on top of the mushrooms. Pour over the white sauce and sprinkle the cheese over the top. Season with salt and pepper. Bake in a moderate oven (350 degrees) for about 30 minutes or until the fillets are tender and the top brown.
Makes 4 servings.

Lobster in Shells

1 lobster
1 cup white sauce
¼ lb. grated cheese, divided
salt and pepper
½ cup light cream

Remove all meat from the lobster. Make sure the shell is intact as the fish is served in the half shells. Add the lobster meat to the sauce and half the cheese. Season with salt and pepper. Place the mixture back into the cleaned shells. Pour the cream over the fish and sprinkle with the remaining cheese. Bake in hot oven until hot enough and cheese is bubbly on top. Serve with fresh crusty bread.
Makes 4 to 6 servings.

Tweed Salmon

About 2 lbs. salmon
1 cup water or fish stock (if not enough liquid from wine)
¼ cup chopped shallots or chives
sweet white wine
salt and pepper
parsley

Place salmon in enough water or stock to cover. Poach gently for about 5-10 minutes. Cool. Flake the meat off the bones. Place in an ovenproof serving dish. Sprinkle shallots over and cover with the wine. Season with salt and pepper and parsley. Bake for about 30 minutes in a moderate oven (350 degrees). Serve hot or cold. If serving cold, serve with a cucumber sauce.

Makes 4 servings.

Fried Sprats

1 lb. Sprats
salt and pepper
1 beaten egg
2 tablespoons fine breadcrumbs
oil to fry

Clean sprats and take out the backbone. Discard the heads. Wash well and dry thoroughly. Season with salt and pepper. Dip in the egg and then the breadcrumbs. Fry in hot oil for 4-5 minutes until browned. Drain well. Serve hot.

Makes 4 servings.

Kedgeree

1 cup uncooked rice
approximately 1 lb. of smoked haddock
4 hard-boiled eggs
salt and pepper
small cup of light cream
parsley (to garnish)

Cook the rice until soft but not soggy. Cook the fish until tender. Chop the eggs into quarters. Drain rice, season well with salt and pepper. Flake fish and pour cream over the rice and fish. Add the chopped eggs and sprinkle the parsley over the top. Serve hot.

Makes 4 to 6 servings.

WALES

Eog wedi ei Bobi (Baked Salmon)

4 lb. salmon
pinch of rosemary
nutmeg
salt and pepper
a few cloves
1 teaspoon vinegar
1 teaspoon lemon juice
1 stick butter

Clean the fish. Rub inside and out with the mixed seasonings. Grease a large oven proofed dish and place the fish in it. Cover with dots of butter and roast in a moderate oven for 20 minutes to the pound. Baste frequently. Serve on a warmed dish with wedges of lemon.

Makes 6 to 8 servings.

Stewed Eels

Buy an eel already gutted from the fishmonger. Cut off the head and throw away. Remove the backbone. Into a large stew pan—put in the eel—put in whole and just shape into a round in the pan. Cover with cold water, add some sea salt and black pepper. Pour in a cupful of white vinegar or white wine, cook very gently over a low heat for about an hour.

When cooled, remove from the pan and cut into thickish slices. Eat with Pembrokeshire new potatoes and fresh brown bread.

Mussel Stew

Approx. 2 quarts mussels
2 small onions, finely grated
1 clove garlic, crushed
2 tablespoons butter
½ cup small button mushrooms, sliced
½ cup white breadcrumbs
1 teaspoon lemon juice
1 teaspoon chopped fresh parsley
salt and pepper
½ glass sweet madeira wine
1 cup water
egg yolk
¼ cup fresh cream

Wash and clean the mussels. Place in a saucepan of water and cook for 5 minutes or till the shells are open. Strain the liquid and reserve. Break up the mussel shells and remove the beards. Fry the onion and garlic in the butter and mushrooms if using. Add the breadcrumbs, lemon juice, parsley, salt and pepper, madeira, and 1 cup water. Simmer for about 3-4 minutes but do not boil. Now add the egg yolk and cream (mixed together) stir in the mussels. Heat but do not boil as egg will curdle. Mussels are a firm favourite in the Swansea area and the market there is famous for its fresh fish supplies.

Makes 6 servings.

Pastai Gocos (Cockle Pie)

The Gower area is the home of the shellfish of Wales. This is only one of the hundreds of recipes from that area.

Pastry:

12 oz. short crust pastry
just enough milk to glaze

Pie filling:

5 cups cockles
¾ lb. streaky bacon, fried and cut up
1 cup cockle stock
2 small white onions, chopped
2 shallots, cut up
salt and pepper

Clean the cockles. Place in large pan and cover with water. Boil till the shells open. Remove the cockles from the shells. Keep some of the cockle stock. Combine all pie filling ingredients in stock pot and heat for 5 to 10 minutes.

Line pie dish with pastry. Fill with filling mixture and seal top. Glaze with milk. Bake in moderate to hot oven (375 degrees) for 30-45 minutes. Serve hot or cold.

Makes 6 servings.

Cig Moch a Brithyll (Bacon & Trout)

8 medium-sized trout
16 slices bacon
salt and pepper
1 tablespoon butter

Clean the fish and remove the bones. Grease an oven proofed dish. Line the base with half the bacon slices. Place trout on top and cover with the remaining bacon. Season with salt and pepper. Dot with butter. Bake in a hot oven (425 degrees) for 20 minutes. Serves 8.

Main Courses

<u>BRETON</u>

Veal Rolls

2 lbs. veal (pound very thin)
1 lb. chopped lean bacon
1 cup chopped onion
2 cloves garlic, crushed
2 tablespoons chopped fresh parsley
salt and black pepper
pinch thyme
1 bay leaf
2 tablespoons butter
1 cup white wine, divided
¼ cup flour
1 cup chicken broth

Cut meat into eight square pieces and pound to about $1/16$-inch. Mix bacon, onions, garlic, parsley, salt and pepper, thyme, and bay leaf together and place a small amount of the mixture on the veal squares. Roll and tie with string. Melt butter in a pan and brown the rolls. Place onto the bottom of an oven dish. Pour half of the wine over rolls and cook in a moderate to hot oven for about ¾ hour or until meat is tender. Make a gravy with the remaining wine, flour, and chicken stock. Season and serve poured over the rolls. These rolls are delicious if served with red cabbage and sour cream.

Makes 4 to 6 servings.

Beef in Red Wine

1 lb. lean beef
½ lb. lean bacon
2 tablespoons butter
2 onions
flour
½ bottle (12.7 oz.) red wine
salt
pepper
thyme
parsley
bay leaf
12 (small) pickling onions

Cut beef and bacon into chunks. Fry in melted butter in a saucepan. When meat is sealed, cut 2 onions into slices and add to the meat. Stir in two spoonfuls of flour; mix well and add one glass of water and half a bottle of red wine, a little at a time. Add salt, pepper, one stalk thyme, parsley and one bay leaf and allow to boil gently for at least 4 hours. If desired, pickling onions may be added 1 hour before serving. Serve hot with jacket potatoes boiled in water.

Makes 4 servings.

Brittany Chicken

2 lbs. small onions, peeled and chopped
2 tablespoons butter
1 large roasting chicken (5 lbs.)
salt and pepper
2 cups water/white wine
¼ cup plain flour

Fry onions in the butter until golden. Clean the fat off the chicken and season outside with salt and pepper. Stuff the inside with the onions. Secure the skin with a thread. Place in a roasting dish and cook for about 1½-2 hours, with the wine/water poured around it. Thicken the liquid with some flour and season. Serve with new potatoes, carrots and green salad.

Makes 4 to 6 servings.

Cheese Soufflé

3 tablespoons butter
¼ cup flour
salt and pepper
1½ cups milk
1 teaspoon mustard
3 oz. grated cheese
cayenne pepper
6 eggs, separated
1 tablespoon breadcrumbs

Grease and prepare the soufflé dish. Melt the butter: add flour and the salt and pepper. Add milk and whisk to a smooth paste. When slightly cooled add the mustard, cheese, cayenne pepper and egg yolks. In a large bowl whisk egg whites until stiff. Fold into the sauce mixture, top with breadcrumbs, and bake in hot oven (425 degrees) for 30 minutes. Serve immediately.

Makes 4 servings.

Onion, Nettle and Cheese Bake

flour to thicken and coat vegetables
1 lb. onions (cut in rings)
½ lb. finely chopped and blanched nettle tops
1 stick butter
2 garlic cloves (chopped very finely)
1 can (28 ounces) whole tomatoes (without the juice) or 6 medium sized skinned tomatoes
2 cups cheese sauce
½ lb. (8 ounces) mild cheese to cover the top of the bake

Fry the flour coated onion rings and nettles with the butter, brown very lightly. Add garlic and cook for a few minutes only. Transfer to a pie dish. Put in the tomatoes—add the sauce and cover with the cheese. Bake in a hot oven (425 degrees) for 1 hour or until browned on top and onions soft.

Makes 4 to 6 servings.

CORNISH

Devon Pork and Cider

1 lb. pork fillet
1/3 cup flour
½ stick butter
4 small cooking apples, peeled and chopped
1 stick celery, chopped
½ lb. onions, chopped
salt and pepper
pinch cinnamon
2 cups sweet cider
1/3 cup cream
parsley

Cut the meat into cubes, and toss in the flour. Heat the butter in a large pan, and add the meat: gently brown. Add the apples, celery, onions, salt and pepper, cinnamon, and cider. Transfer to an ovenproof dish. Cook in moderate oven (350 degrees) for about one hour. Just before serving stir in the cream. Sprinkle with chopped parsley.

Makes 4 servings.

Main Courses

Cornish Pasty

1 lb. shortcrust pastry
1 lb. lean trimmed mutton
3 good sized potatoes (chopped)
2 medium onions, chopped
2 medium carrots, chopped
pinch chopped parsley
pinch chopped fresh herbs (assorted)
salt and pepper
milk for glazing

Make the pastry and chill for about an hour before using. Chop up the meat finely, mix in the chopped vegetables with the meat, herbs and season well. Roll out pastry to a large round. Place meat and vegetable mixture in the centre. Bring over one side of the pastry to form a half round. Crimp edges and glaze with milk. Bake in a moderately hot oven (375 degrees) for 1 hour. Filling for a Cornish pasty should always be raw. This Cornish pasty can be made as one large one or several small ones. In Cornwall they were eaten by the Tin and Copper miners at "Crib" time.
Makes 4 servings.

Lamb Kidneys

12 young kidneys
flour to coat
salt and pepper
½ stick butter (to fry)
2 medium sized onions, chopped
½ cup meat stock
1 cup sweet white wine

Clean kidneys. Toss in the flour and salt and pepper. Fry in the hot butter with onions until browned. Add stock and wine, cook for approximately 10 minutes until cooked. Serve with new spring potatoes.
Makes 4 servings.

Nettles, Onion and Spinach Pie

1 lb. nettle tips
1 lb. fresh spinach or 1 box (10 ounces) frozen spinach
2 medium–sized onions, well chopped
Salt and pepper
4 small eggs (well beaten)
½ lb. good strong cheese, grated

Choose any young nettles and use only the tips. Pick them and cook for 10 minutes. Squeeze all the water from them and chop up small. Do the same with spinach, but drain well.

Put the nettles, spinach, and onions in a high sided pie dish. Sprinkle with salt and pepper. Add eggs, cheese on the top - cover with foil and place dish in a dish of water to come half way up the sides. Bake in moderate oven (350 degrees) for 1-1¼ hours. Eat warm with crusty bread.

Makes 4 servings.

Main Courses

<u>MANX</u>

Isle of Man Hot Pot

Large neck of mutton
1 lb. onions, chopped
2 lbs. potatoes, chopped
½ lb. leeks, chopped
½ lb. carrots, chopped
salt and pepper

Place meat on base of large pot. Cover over and around with the vegetables. Season with salt and pepper and cover with water. Simmer gently for 3 - 3½ hours.
Makes 4 to 6 servings.

Sollaghan

Take a basinful of oatmeal. Put meal into oven or in pan on fire and keep turning meal until it is crisped to a reddish color. Put meal into a dish: add salt and pepper and a lump of butter to flavor. Then put 2-3 basinfuls of stock or broth upon the meal and mix until it sticks together in lumps. Fill up dish with broth until enough to serve into plates upon the table to eat. This makes a very wholesome meal. Sollaghan was traditionally served on the Island on Christmas morning.

Layered Dinner

Place the following into a deep casserole in the following order.
Approximately 1 inch layer of peeled and sliced potatoes. Peeled and diced carrots. Peel and sliced red onions and chopped savoy cabbage. Mixture of swede and turnip, chopped into smallish cubes. 8-10 rashers of fairly thick bacon. Layer of peeled and sliced parsnips. Good handful of white rice. Season well with salt and pepper. Enough good meat

stock to keep moist. Over the top of the pie, cover with strong grated cheese. Cook for 2 hours in a moderate oven Cover the casserole for the first hour of cooking then leave open to brown.

A very easy and tasty dish. Eat with fresh bread and butter.

Roast Chicken with Sage and Onion Stuffing

1 roasting fowl
3 potatoes, quartered
3 carrots, cut in 1-inch pieces
3 medium onions, quartered

Stuffing:

¼ lb. stale bread (crumbled)
little water
2 large onions, chopped
pinch sage
salt and pepper
½ stick butter

Clean the chicken and remove the insides. To prepare stuffing: Pour some water over the bread to soak. Combine chopped onions with the sage and season with salt and pepper. Add the bread and butter and mash together thoroughly. Stuff the fowl and arrange in a large roasting pan. Arrange potatoes, carrots, and onions around the fowl. Bake in moderate oven (350 degrees) for 15 minutes to the pound and fifteen minutes over. Serve with roast carrots, potatoes and a green vegetable. Make gravy with the fowl juices from the roasting pan.

Makes 6 to 8 servings.

Sausage Casserole

8 large pork sausages
flour to thicken
salt and pepper
4 good sized onions—chopped finely
stock to cover the meats
1 glass red wine or Port

Prick sausages and cover in flour. Season with salt and pepper to taste. Fry until lightly browned. Add onions, stock and wine. Cook in a covered casserole on top of the stove for 1 hour on low heat.

Makes 6 to 8 servings.

IRISH

Colcannon

This is one of the traditional Irish dishes using the much favored potato. It was often served on Halloween and also as a supper dish of "First Kettling Night"—the first day that friends visited the home of a newly married couple.

4 tablespoons dripping
1 lb. cooked mashed potatoes
½ lb. cabbage, shredded
½ lb. onions (chopped)
½ lb. bacon (about 15 slices), cut into small cubes
salt and pepper
pinch of parsley

Melt the dripping and add the potatoes, cabbage, and onions. Cook until browned. Add the bacon and cook. Season with salt and pepper. Serve on a large platter with parsley sprinkled over the top.

Makes 4 to 6 servings.

Irish Stew

2 lb. neck of mutton
3 lb. potatoes
1 lb. onions
1 cup stock
salt and pepper

Cube the meat and cup up the vegetables into small pieces. Place in a large saucepan and add the stock. Season with salt and pepper. Simmer for 3 hours. The meat used in the original Irish Stew was, I gather, that of a goat or kid, but now it seems to be mutton that is used for this very old Irish dish.

Makes 4 to 6 servings.

The Tinker's Dinner

How this recipe came by its odd name I do not know. Maybe it was because the Irish tinkers are supposed to be very light fingered! This dish is now served at festivals, like Harvest time and of course Christmas time.

1 turkey

Stuffing:

1 lb. dry breadcrumbs
1 lb. onions, diced
4 tablespoons mashed potatoes
pinch of sage
½ teaspoon salt
½ teaspoon black pepper
1 beaten egg
water to mix

Mix all the stuffing ingredients thoroughly and put into the turkey. Secure the back and tail so that the stuffing does not ooze out. Place the turkey in a roasting dish and brush with melted butter. Cook for 15-20 minutes to the lb. in a moderate oven (350 degrees). This dish can be served with potato pancakes:

1 lb. grated raw potatoes
2 small onions, chopped
2 beaten eggs
⅓ cup flour
salt and pepper

Mix the potato, onion, eggs and flour together. Season with salt and pepper. Shape into fritters. Fry until cooked a golden brown.
Makes 10 to 12 servings.

Brawn

1 pig's head
1 pig's trotter
1 sheep's tongue
½ lb. good stewing beef
1 lb. belly pork

Soak the pig's head overnight in salted water. Next day cover with water and cook all the meats together until very tender. Skin the tongue. Chop up all the meats together. Place in an oblong type lunch box (pottery) and strain some of the liquids that the meats were cooked in over and leave to set. Cut in slices when set.

Makes 6 to 8 servings.

Bacon and Onion Roly Poly

The Suet Pastry:

2 cups self-rising flour
¼ lb. shredded suet
½ cup water
1 lb. bacon (about 15 slices), finely chopped
2 onions, chopped
2 apples, chopped and peeled
pinch of salt, pepper and sage

Mix flour, suet, and water together. Roll out the pastry into an oblong shape. Lay the bacon, onion, apple and seasonings on the pastry. Carefully roll over and dampen the edges (to seal) wrap in a greased paper and foil—steam for approximately 2½-3 hours.

Makes 4 to 6 servings.

SCOTLAND

Aberdeen Sausage

1 lb. stewing steak (minced)
15 slices bacon, minced
1 cup rolled oats
1 tablespoon Worcestershire sauce
1 cup seasoned breadcrumbs
1 beaten egg

Mix the steak, bacon, oats, Worcestershire sauce, and breadcrumbs together. Bind with the egg. Make into a roll. Bake in a moderate oven (350 degrees) for about 1½-2 hours or until meat is cooked through. Leave to cool. Use next day, sliced with a salad.

Makes 6 to 8 servings.

Scotch Eggs

6 hard-boiled eggs (shelled)
breadcrumbs
1 lb. sausage meat
salt and pepper
oil or fat for frying

Cover the eggs with the breadcrumbs. Cut up the seasoned sausage meat into 6 sections. Cover each egg with enough of the meat. Season with salt and pepper. Fry in deep fat. Serve hot or cold.

Makes 6 servings.

Haggis

the liver, heart and lights of one sheep
½ lb. suet
large cup of fine oatmeal
2 large onions
salt and pepper
few drops of milk

Put the liver, heart, suet, etc. in a large pan and cover with water. Simmer for 1½ hours. Toast the oatmeal. Cool the meats. When cold, mince meats roughly. Chop onions and mix in the oatmeal. Season with salt and pepper. Add a little milk if too dry. Place in a large basin. Cover with foil and steam for about 3-4 hours. Serve hot.

Stovies

about 1 lb. potatoes
left over cold meat
1 small onion, diced
4 tablespoons dripping
salt and pepper
¾ cup water or stock
chopped fresh parsley

Cut the potatoes into cubes. Place meat, diced onion and potatoes in a pan with the dripping. Season with salt and pepper. Add water or stock. Cover and cook for 10-15 minutes on a low heat. Serve with fresh parsley sprinkled over the top. This is one way the Scots have of using up cold meat. It's a good supper dish on a cold winter's night.
Makes 4 to 6 servings.

WALES

Potes Mis Medi (Harvest Hot Pot)

2 tablespoons butter
15 slices bacon, cut into pieces
½ lb. cubed lamb (uncooked)
¼ cup wheaten flour
1 lb. potatoes, peeled and cubed
1 lb. carrots, peeled and cubed
1 lb. onions, chopped
4 leeks, chopped
½ lb. swedes or turnips, chopped
salt and pepper
4 cups water

In a large pot, melt the butter, fry and brown meats, adding the flour to thicken. Add the vegetables, salt and pepper, and water. Simmer gently for two hours. Serve with fresh brown bread. This is a complete meal in one pot. This dish was often used during the potato picking season in Wales as it was easily made and left on the hook over the open fire to keep hot. The pickers were often late in to their dinners—often from chatting—not from picking the potatoes. There used to be a school holiday in Wales called Wythnos Hela Tatws (Potato Picking Week).

Makes 8 servings.

Ham in Cider

The ham should be soaked overnight in cold water.

5-6 lb. piece of ham
1 large onion
8 cloves
2½ cups cider and water (½ quantities of each)
juice of 1 lemon
pinch of brown sugar

Place the ham into a large stewpan. Prick the onion with the cloves: add all other ingredients. Bring to the boil and simmer slowly for 25-30 minutes, to each pound. Cool, then peel off the skin.

Mix together:

3 tablespoons brown sugar
3 tablespoons breadcrumbs
1 teaspoon made mustard
¼ teaspoon mace
¼ teaspoon nutmeg

Press the mixture into the harp and place into a greased pie dish. Bake for 40-50 minutes in moderate oven. Serve with vegetables or salad. Can also be served with the traditional parsley sauce.
Makes 6 to 8 servings.

Ffagots

2 lbs. of either calf's, pig's or lamb's liver
5 oz. finely chopped suet
¾ cup oatmeal or breadcrumbs
3 large onions (minced)
2 teaspoons salt
¼ teaspoon black pepper
pinch each of nutmeg, sage, thyme, mace

Place all the ingredients into a large bowl and mix very thoroughly. Grease a large meat tin and place mixture into this. Cover the top with pork flat pieces.

Cook in a slow oven (300 degrees) for about an hour. After 30 minutes mark top of meat into squares. Leave to get cold in the tin. Can be eaten cold or hot. This recipe was much used by the families of miners, as the fagots were so easily transportable in their miners "tocyn" (lunch). They also provided vital nourishment for the strenuous work of mining.
Makes 6 servings.

Ffest y Cybydd

1 lb. potatoes
1 large rutabaga
4 onions
½ lb. carrots
1 leek
15 slices streaky bacon
salt and pepper
1 cup stock

Cut up the potatoes, rutabaga, onions, and carrots into slices. Dice the leek and bacon. Place alternative layers of bacon and the vegetables. Season to taste with salt and pepper. Pour stock over. Bake in a moderate oven (350 degrees) for 1 hour.
This dish, with fresh bread, was often served at my home.
Makes 6 servings.

Glamorgan Sausages

3 cups grated cheese
6 cups fine breadcrumbs
1 tablespoon dry mustard
salt and pepper to season
2 large onions (minced)
2 teaspoon fresh herbs (if not available use dried herbs)
3 large eggs (well beaten)
flour to coat (before frying)
oil or lard for frying

Mix up all the first 6 ingredients. Make a well and pour in the beaten eggs, mix well. Form into small sausages. Coat in flour and fry in oil until browned.

Makes 6 servings.

Gwydd y Dolig

12-14 lb. goose
4 tablespoons red wine, maderia or port
8 slices streaky bacon

The stuffing:

1 cup white breadcrumbs
2 apples, peeled and chopped
2 small onions, peeled and chopped
1 egg
salt and pepper
pinch sage and nutmeg

Make the stuffing by combining all ingredients thoroughly. Stuff the goose and secure with a steel skewer or sew with tacking thread. Place the bird in a large baking tin. Pour over wine or port and roast in a moderate oven (350 degrees) for 20-25 minutes to the pound. Baste often to keep moist. About ½ hour before cooking is complete place strips of bacon across the bird and leave till being served. Make in a criss-cross pattern. This recipe is usually served with an apple sauce (as goose is a fairly fatty meat).

Sauce:

¾ lb. sharp cooking apples, peeled and chopped
2 small onions, chopped
3 tablespoons sugar
pinch mustard, salt and pepper
small pinch nutmeg and cinnamon
¾ cup cider
3 tablespoons breadcrumbs

Cook the apples and onions, sugar, mustard, salt and pepper, nutmeg and cinnamon in the cider. When vegetables are soft add breadcrumbs. Simmer gently for a few seconds. Serve in a gravy boat alongside the goose gravy.

This dish is served at Christmastime but occasionally at such events as christenings and weddings too.

Makes 12 or more servings.

The goose is a popular bird to keep on the small holdings in Wales, as apart from the meat the bird provides, the feathers are used for the down quilts and in years gone by the filling of the feather beds.

The long wing pinion was used for sweeping the hearth and I can recall my grandmother using one in her farm when I was young.

Salted Duck

The duck must be salted one day before being cooked.

1 large duck
1 lb. small onions, chopped
½ cup milk
2 tablespoons butter
¼ cup flour
salt and pepper

Place the duck in a pot and cover with water. Simmer slowly for 1½-2 hours, depending on size. Boil the onion in the milk till tender. Make a

roux sauce by melting butter, stir in flour and salt and pepper and add to milk and onions. Drain the duck and place on a large platter. Pour over sauce. Serve with new Pembrokeshire boiled potatoes, carrots and a green vegetable. This is a very old and a traditional Welsh recipe.
Makes 6 servings.

Twrci Mewn Blanced

Make a quantity of hot water pastry with the following ingredients:

2 cups flour
¾ cup milk
pinch of salt
4 tablespoons lard
¾ cup water

Ingredients for the shell filling:

1 lb. cold turkey—cut up in small cubes
4 small onions, chopped
1 leek, chopped
1 carrot, chopped
1 rutabaga or turnip, chopped
4 potatoes, chopped
salt and pepper to taste
1 cup good giblet stock

Line a dish with the warm pastry. Place into the shell the diced turkey meat, onion and the other vegetables cut up small, add salt and pepper and stock. Seal the case and bake in moderate oven till browned and vegetables cooked. About 1 hour. Serves 4. This is a favourite dish in Cardiganshire to use up the Christmas turkey.
Makes 6 servings.

Game

BRETON

Rabbit with Mushrooms

1 medium sized fresh rabbit
½ stick butter
⅓ cup all-purpose flour
1 lb. mushrooms (cleaned and sliced)
1 lb. small white onions, chopped
1 clove garlic (crushed or chopped)
2 cups white wine
salt and pepper
chopped parsley

Cut up rabbit into about six pieces. Melt the butter and brown the rabbit pieces. Thicken the fat with the flour when meat is browned. Add mushrooms, onions, garlic, white wine, and salt and pepper, and cook until rabbit meat is tender in a slow oven (300 degrees). Serve sprinkled with chopped parsley.

Makes 6 servings.

Quail in Red Wine

8 quails
½ stick butter
½ cup sherry
1 cup red wine
1 cup beef stock
black pepper
salt
⅓ cup plain flour
a few grapes to decorate

Clean the birds. Tie the birds across their breasts with a piece of white string—this keeps them in shape whilst cooking. Melt the butter and brown the quails. Transfer to a large casserole and add the sherry, red wine, stock, and pepper and salt. Cook until tender in a moderate oven with the lid on for all but the last 30 minutes or so. Thicken the gravy juices with the flour and serve hot garnished with grapes. At least two quails per person is needed as they are very tiny birds.

Makes 4 servings.

Wild Roast Duck

Truss the bird for roasting. Bake in a large baking dish after sprinkling it well with strong seasoned flour. Baste all over with hot fat and cook for about 20-30 minutes in a moderate hot oven (375 degrees). Do not overcook as the flavors are then lost. Serve with a good orange sauce or other sharp fruits.

Game Pie

hot water pastry (see recipe page 69)
1 lb. of uncooked pigeon, pheasant, partridge meats
4 slices streaky bacon
½ lb. good stewing steak, cubed
½ lb. minced venison meat
2 onions, chopped
pinch mixed herbs
salt and pepper
1 cup good stock, divided
1 small beaten egg (for glazing)
2 teaspoons gelatin powder

Roll out the pastry bottom to cover a pie dish. Line the inside with the various meats. Put onions on the top. Season well with mixed herbs and salt and pepper. Add the herbs. Add half the stock. Put a cover over the pie and make a slit for the steam to come out, and glaze with beaten egg. Bake for about 2½ hours in a hot oven (425 degrees). Cover pie with greased paper to stop browning too much. When pie is cooked remove from the oven. Combine remaining stock with gelatin. Gently pour this mixture into the pie through the steam hole. Refrigerate the pie. Remove from dish and serve cold, cut into slices with salads.

Makes 6 servings.

Pigeon Casserole

Breast meat of 6 pigeons, cubed or shredded
2 large onions, chopped
salt and pepper
1 teaspoon of mace and ground cinnamon
1 cup dry wine
1 cup port
flour (to thicken)

Put everything in a casserole and mix thoroughly. Cook slowly for 2 hours at 300 degrees. Serve with roasted vegetables (potatoes, carrots, and parsnips).

Makes 6 servings.

CORNISH

Rabbit Hoggan

Pastry:

> 1 lb. (18 cups) plain flour
> ¾ cup lard
> salt
> drop of lemon juice
> enough water to mix

For the filling:

> 1 lb. rabbit meat, chopped into small pieces (the rabbit must be young and fresh)
> 6 potatoes (small)
> 2 carrots
> 2 onions
> 2 small turnips
> salt and pepper
> little amount of stock

Make the pastry and roll out to a round. Cut up the meat and vegetables into small cubes. Place the vegetables and meat in the middle of the pastry round. Season with salt and pepper and just put a little stock over. Seal the pastry and stand it on its base on a balking tray. Crimp the edges and brush with milk. Bake for about 1-1½ hours in a moderate oven (350 degrees), or as the contents are uncooked maybe a little longer. This amount makes one huge hoggan or 6 smaller ones.

Makes 6 servings.

Jugged Hare

Jugged Hare was often served in the West Country on Boxing Day.

1 large glass sweet cider
1 large glass white vinegar
salt and pepper
bay leaf
1 onion, sliced
4 carrots
3 small onions
½ stick butter
flour for dredging
4 slices streaky bacon
2 small glasses of red wine
little drop of port
approx. 2 cups good brown stock (or use the marinade)
2 oz. arrowroot
2 tablespoons red currant jelly

Hang the hare for 3-4 days. Joint the hare and cut into serving-size pieces. The day before it is to be cooked, place hare pieces in a marinade of cider, vinegar, salt and pepper, and bay leaf. Peel and chop the vegetables. Melt butter and brown vegetables. Coat hare in flour, add to the pan. Cook until slightly browned. Transfer vegetables to a large pie dish. Place hare pieces on top. Place bacon slices over hare pieces. Pour wines and stock over and cook with the lid on for about 3 hours in a moderate oven. Thicken with the arrowroot if the sauce is too thin. Just before serving add red currant jelly.

Makes 6 to 8 servings.

Flamed Wild Duck with Port Sauce

1 medium sized wild duck
small glass brandy
salt and pepper
6 shallot heads
6 oz. mushrooms
small amount of good white sauce

Roast the duck until cooked. When the duck is cooled, take out of the oven and drain off any fat. Carve all the flesh off the bird and place in a casserole dish, pur over the brandy and set alight. When burnt off, add the salt and pepper, shallots, mushrooms and the white sauce. Cover and cook in a hot oven (425 degrees) for 30 minutes. Serve with croutons of fried bread and slivers of roasted carrots, parsnips and a green salad.

Sauce:

2 tablespoons butter
¼ cup flour
½ cup stock
salt and pepper
pinch of mace

Make a roux of butter and flour. Add stock and boil well. Add salt and pepper and mace. Serve very hot.

Roasted Grouse

one bird per person
Hang for 3-4 days. Pluck and draw as for chicken. Cover the breasts completely with streaky bacon. Roast for about ¾ hour—baste frequently with hot fat. About 15 minutes before the end of the cooking time, shake seasoned flour all over the breasts. Pour fat over the birds and this time brown nicely for serving. Serve hot on savouries of toast. Very fattening!

Squab Pie (Young Pigeons)

1 lb. shortcrust pastry
breast meat of 2 pigeons per person
¼ lb. onions, chopped
¼ lb. apples, chopped
salt and pepper
pinch ginger
½ cup good white stock

Line the bottom of the pie dish with half the pastry. Layer the meats, onion and apples until filled. Add salt and pepper and ginger and pour over stock. Put a lid on the pie and cook for about 2 hours in a moderately hot oven (375 degrees).

Makes 4 servings.

MANX

Ragout of Wild Duck

2 tablespoons butter
2 breasts of duck per person (meat removed from bones)
1 onion, chopped
4 shallots
¼ cup flour
salt and pepper
1 small glass orange juice
1 small glass of dry sherry

Melt the butter, add the duck meat, chopped onion and shallots. Dredge with flour. Cook carefully until well browned. Add salt and pepper, orange juice and sherry and simmer very gently for about an hour. (Do not boil.)

Makes 4 servings.

Roasted Stuffed Rabbit

Weigh the rabbit and roast for 15 minutes per lb. and 15 minutes over.

Stuffing:
Enough bread, onions, finely chopped prunes and seasonings to fill the belly cavity. Prepare the stuffing and put into the rabbit. Sew securely.

Place in a baking tin. Cover with flour and put strips of bacon over it in a criss-cross pattern. Pour over some melted butter. Roast at about 180 degrees F. Baste with its own juices regularly. Serve with warmed red currant jelly.

Grouse Pie

½ lb. grouse meat
½ lb. good stewing steak
½ lb. carrots
4 onions
butter to fry
flour to coat meats
pinch of nutmeg
salt and pepper
enough stock to make moist
½ lb. flaky pastry

Cut up meats. Chop vegetables. Melt butter. Dredge with flour. Fry meats and vegetables gently. Place in a casserole dish, add nutmeg, salt and pepper, and stock. Take out. Put a pastry lid on top. Cook until pastry is golden brown.

Makes 4 to 6 servings.

Roast Snipe

1 snipe per person
melted butter
seasoned flour

Lay on their backs in a roasting dish. Dredge all over with the flour. Pour over the melted butter. Roast for about 10-15 minutes or until cooked through. Serve with a good onion gravy.

Game Pie

½ lb. good sausage meat
8 slices streaky bacon
3 onions, chopped
few mushrooms, sliced
½ lb. cooked wild duck, shredded
few tomatoes
3 hard-boiled eggs
salt and pepper
2 tablespoons red currant sauce
enough stock to just moisten the meats
enough shortcrust pastry to line the pie dish

Cook the sausage meat and bacon. Add the onions and mushrooms. Cook for a few minutes. Line the pie dish with bottom crust. Put the sausage mixture into the pie dish along with the duck. Add the tomatoes and slice the eggs and place on the top. Season well with salt and pepper. Add the red currant sauce and stock. Put top crust on the pie. Cook in a moderate hot oven (375 degrees) until the pastry is well cooked. Cool. Serve in slices with a salad.

Makes 6 servings.

IRISH

Roast Grouse

½ lb. stewing meat (beef preferably)
2 young grouse
½ stick butter
8 slices streaky bacon
salt and pepper

Cut the steak into four equal pieces. Wash and dry the grouse and put the steak inside the birds (2 pieces in each bird). Place the grouse in a buttered dish to roast and put the bacon strips over them. Season with salt and pepper. Roast in a moderate oven (350 degrees) for about an hour. Serve the steak together with the birds.
Makes 4 servings.

Roasted Hare

The time for roasting a young hare is about 20 minutes to the pound.
Prepare the hare and remove its head. Leave a longish piece of neck skin for trussing and to keep the stuffing in. Stuff the hare with the following:

½ cup white breadcrumbs
½ stick butter
salt and pepper
1 beaten egg
2 medium onions, chopped
pinch of sage and thyme

Add these together and use for the stuffing. Sew the hare with a thick cotton which can be easily removed before serving. Place hare in a roasting dish; cover with strips of bacon. Cook in a moderate oven. Serve with roast carrots and potatoes and a gravy made from the roasted hare juices.

Roast Pheasant

1 small pheasant per person
1 onion (to put inside each bird)
2 slices streaky bacon
flour to coat
salt and pepper
½ stick butter (melted)
watercress to garnish

Put birds in a roasting dish. Quarter the onion and insert in bird's cavity. Cover breasts with bacon. Dredge with flour, salt and pepper. Pour butter over the birds. Cook in a moderate oven (350 degrees) for about 10-15 minutes per lb. Garnish with watercress and serve with game chips.
Makes one serving.

Potted Hare

Cut up a cooked roasted hare into small pieces and mince finely. Mince also a small cooked onion. Mix together and add seasonings to taste, add a pinch of mace and enough gravy to moisten. Pour some melted butter into small pots swirl round to coat. Press in the mixture well. Add more melted butter to cover the top. Cover with muslin.

Stewed Rabbit

1 rabbit
½ stick butter
⅓ cup flour
½ lb. potatoes
½ lb. onions
½ lb. leeks
½ lb. carrots
½ lb. turnips
2 cups stock
salt and pepper
chopped parsley

Cut the rabbit into 6 portions. Melt the butter. Coat the rabbit pieces in flour. Fry until browned. Cut up the vegetables and place over the meat in a large stewpot. Add stock and season with salt and pepper. Cook slowly for about 2 hours. Garnish with chopped parsley.

Serve this stew with some dumplings and it is a complete meal in one pot.

½ stick butter
⅓ cup flour
salt
2 eggs
1 cup boiling water (if not boiling in the stew)

Melt the butter. Add to the flour and salt. Beat the eggs and add to the dry mixture. Roll into small balls. Cook in the boiling water or add to the stew about 10 minutes before serving. These are better tasting if cooked in the stewpot.

SCOTLAND

Scotsman Casserole

brace of grouse
½ stick butter
2 small carrots (diced)
2 small onions (chopped)
½ lb. fried mushrooms (sliced)
4 slices bacon
salt and pepper
½ cup red wine
½ cup water

Prepare the grouse and cut in half. Heat butter in a large pan and brown birds well. Place in an ovenproof casserole and add carrots, onions, mushrooms and bacon (chopped). Season with salt and pepper. Add the wine and water. Cook in moderate oven (350 degrees) for 2-2½ hours or until tender. Thicken the gravy before serving with flour, if needed.
Makes 4 to 6 servings.

Roasted Venison Steaks

oil and butter to fry
16 small onions
4 venison steaks (approximately 6 oz. in weight)

Sauce:

½ cup medium cream sherry
4 tablespoons cranberry sauce
2 teaspoons coarse grained mustard
¼ cup single cream

Mix the first three sauce ingredients and simmer slowly until well mixed. Add the oil/butter mixture to a heavy based frypan. Heat until hot. Fry whole onions until brown and almost cooked. Add steaks and cook for about 5 minutes on each side. Before serving the sauce add the cream but do not boil. Just heat until hot. Pour over venison.

Makes 4 servings.

Quail with Prunes

Allow one bird per person. Clean and truss. Wrap all around with bacon slices. Place some soft prunes over the breast area of the bird. Wrap in foil and cook in a hot oven (425 degrees) for about 15 minutes. Open the foil parcel and cook for a further 10 minutes. Serve with game chips.

Grouse Pudding

3 grouse, chopped
½ lb. chopped bacon
2 carrots, chopped
4 onions, chopped
1 cup good game stock
1 cup red wine
salt and pepper
2 tablespoons butter
¼ cup flour
dash of whiskey

For the top:

½ cup flour
6 tablespoons butter
2 oz. strong cheese

Combine topping ingredients until it forms a bread crumb consistency.

Put all the chopped meats into a casserole. Add carrots, onions, stock, and wine. Season with salt and pepper to taste. Add butter, flour, and dash whiskey. Mix thoroughly. Cook for about 1 hour in a moderate hot oven (375 degrees). Take out and add topping. Cook for another 45 minutes.

Makes 4 to 6 servings.

The Huntsman's Dinner

1 boiling chicken
1 rabbit
2 tablespoons butter
15 slices bacon
¼ cup flour
½ lb. carrots
1 lb. potatoes
½ lb. onions
4 cups stock
salt and pepper
parsley
salt and pepper

Cut up the chicken and rabbit into small portions. Melt butter in a large cook pot. Coat meats and bacon with flour and fry until brown. Cut up vegetables and add to the meat. Add stock. Season with salt and pepper. Cook for about two hours on a simmering heat. Sprinkle with chopped parsley. Serve with a green vegetable.

Makes 10 to 12 servings.

WALES

Montgomeryshire Pheasant

1 pheasant
2 tablespoons butter
1 large onion
1 large carrot
1 large leek
1 turnip
pinch of parsley, thyme
salt and pepper
¼ bottle of red wine
water
¼ cup flour

Prepare the pheasant. Heat the butter in a heavy pan. Lightly fry the bird till browned. Take out and put to one side. Peel and cut up vegetables into small cubes or slices. Place in bottom of pan and add seasonings. Place the pheasant onto the vegetables and cover with wine and water. Place a lid on the pot and simmer slowly for two hours. Thicken with the flour just before serving.

Makes 4 servings.

Pastai Cwningen

Make up short crust pastry using:

1½ cups flour
1 stick butter
1 egg
2 tablespoons water
pinch of salt

Ingredients for crust pastry filling:

butter for browning the meat
1 jointed and cooked rabbit
8 slices bacon, chopped
1 onion, chopped
1 large leek, chopped
salt and pepper
1 pint good stock

Line bottom of a fairly large deep pie dish with the pastry. Heat butter and fry the rabbit till browned all over. Add the bacon, onion and leek, and salt and pepper. Let this cook and when cold, place into pastry case. Add stock and place the crust over the top. Seal and brush with egg or milk. Bake in a moderate oven (350 degrees) for 30 minutes till pastry is browned.

Makes 4 to 6 servings.

Rook Pie

Use only the breast meat (1 lb. approximately). Soak overnight in salted water. Dry and lay layers of the meat and bacon strips in a pie dish. Chop 2 large onions finely and sprinkle over the meats. Season well and add some of the cream from the top of the milk, just enough to cover. Cover with a rich short crust pastry and cook for about 1½ hours. Serve with boiled carrots and mashed rutabaga and potatoes.

Poacher's Casserole

1 lb. boneless rabbit meat
½ lb. bacon pieces
¼ lb. each of pigeon and pheasant meats
butter to fry
2 large leeks or 2 bunches shallots, chopped
salt and pepper
good pinch mixed herbs
flour (to cook the meats)
½ pint dry cider
parsley to garnish

Cut up meats, fry in butter until slightly browned. Add leeks and coat with the seasonings, mixed herbs and flour. Put into a casserole dish. Pour over the cider. Cook until the meat is tender. Sprinkle over parsley before serving.

Makes 6 servings.

Boiled Venison

A piece about 2 lbs. in weight. Marinade for a day in a good meat marniated. Put meat into a large stewpot. Add enough red wine and a good cup of whiskey to cover. Cook slowly. About 45 minutes before end of cooking time, add 2 large onions—Finely chopped—2 large tablespoons honey and a jar of cranberry sauce. Finish the cooking and slice into thick slices. Serve with game chips and vegetables in season.

Sweets

BRETON

French Apple Tart

1 lb. apples
1 cup sugar, divided
1 glass cider brandy
2 cups flour
4 eggs
1 cup milk

Peel and cut apples into thin slices. Place on glass dish and cover with ¾ cup sugar and cider brandy. Allow to stand overnight. The following day, make a batter with the flour, ¼ cup sugar, eggs and milk. Add apples to this batter. Pour the mixture into a well buttered shallow pie-plate and place in medium-hot oven (375 degrees) for one hour.
Makes 6 servings.

Crème Brûlée

1½ cups light cream
2 cups heavy cream
3 tablespoons granulated sugar
6 small egg yolks
5 tablespoons brown sugar

Heat the cream and granulated sugar in a double boiler for 2 minutes. Remove from the heat. Add egg yolks. Stir well. Cook for 5 more minutes. Pour crème brûlée into a wetted mold and chill for at least 6 hours. Just before serving, sprinkle brown sugar over top and grill until melted.
Makes 6 servings.

Sweets

Chocolate Mousse

1 lb. (16 ounces) dark chocolate
8 eggs, separated
3 tablespoons brandy

Melt the chocolate over hot water. Add a drop of water if too thick. Stir to keep smooth. Separate egg yolks and put to one side. Stir yolks into chocolate mixture. Beat whites of eggs until very stiff. Fold the brandy into the chocolate and egg mixture and then the whites of the eggs. Leave to set in a cool place.
Makes 6 to 8 servings.

Pears in Red Wine

6 medium pears
1 cup red wine
¼ cup sugar
pinch of cinnamon
1 teaspoon Tia Maria

Peel and core the fruit. Gently pour in the wine and sugar mixture. Add the cinnamon and liqueur and heat gently. Serve hot.
Makes 6 servings.

Tarte Tatin

The Pastry:

1 stick butter
2 cups all-purpose flour
½ cup confectioners' sugar
3 egg yolks

Rub butter into flour, add icing sugar and egg yolks. Mix to a dough. Chill for several hours. Line a pie dish and bake blind for 35 - 40 mins. Cool.

The Filling:

> 6 large pears (par boiled)
> 1½ cups milk
> 6 egg yolks
> ½ cup granulated sugar
> 2 tablespoonfuls cream
> ¼ cup flour or cornstarch (to thicken)
> a small dollop of Almond Liqueur
> extra sugar for the top (to caramelize)

Peel and par boil pears. Slice thickly. Put milk in a pan, bring to almost a boil. Put yolks in a bowl, add sugar and cream. Add flour. Mix. Pour in milk and heat until smooth. Return all to the pan, boil for a few seconds. Cool and stir in cream and liqueur. Arrange all pears in the pastry case. Pour in the custard mixture. Sprinkle extra sugar on top and heat on high until caramelized.

Makes 6 servings.

CORNISH

Cornish Splits

2 tablespoons sugar
1 tablespoon yeast
2 tablespoons butter
2 tablespoons lard
½ cup milk
½ cup water
4 cups all-purpose flour
pinch salt

Combine the sugar and yeast. Add the butter and lard to the warmed milk and water. Then combine all ingredients with the flour and salt. Make into a dough. Leave to rise in warm place until well risen. Knead and shape into balls. Bake for 20 minutes in hot oven (425 degrees). Serve cold and split in half and fill with cream.

Makes 6 to 8 servings.

Golden Apples

Approximately 1 lb. short crust pastry
1 lb. apples
pinch nutmeg

Roll and cut pastry into 4 small squares. Peel and core apples. Place a quarter of the apples into each small square of pastry. Fold over into a triangle and place in a pie dish. Pour the following mixture over the pastry squares:

1¼ cups boiling water
4 tablespoons light corn syrup
½ cup brown sugar

Mix well: bake in a moderate to hot oven (375 degrees) for 40 minutes. Serve with clotted cream.

Makes 4 servings.

Syllabub

juice of 2 oranges
juice of 2 lemons
4 tablespoons cider
4 tablespoons brandy
pinch of cinnamon
2 cups cream
½ cup granulated sugar

Grate the peel of the fruits and squeeze the juice. Mix with the cider and brandy, sugar and cinnamon and leave overnight. Next day mix in the cream and sugar and chill. Serve with fresh fruit in small glasses.
Makes 6 servings.

Baked Trifle

6 slices stale plain cake, spread with raspberry jam
2 cups milk
2 drops vanilla essence
2 egg yolks
1 teaspoon sugar
2 egg whites
2 tablespoons sugar

Arrange the cake on the bottom of an ovenproof dish. Pour the milk, vanilla and beaten egg yolks over the cake. Sprinkle the teaspoon of sugar over the top. Bake in a moderate oven (350 degrees) for about 1 hour, or until set. Allow to cool. Beat the egg whites until stiff. Mix in 2 tablespoons sugar and pile on top of the baked pudding. Brown in the oven for a few seconds. Serve with cream and fresh fruit.
Makes 6 servings.

Poverty Pudding

2 cups all-purpose flour
½ cup raisins
½ cup golden raisins
2 tablespoons peel
1 teaspoon mixed spice
½ cup sugar
1 teaspoon baking soda
½ cup milk
2 tablespoons dripping
⅓ cup boiling water
2 tablespoons molasses

Sift the flour, add raisins, peel, spice and sugar. Dissolve the baking soda in the milk. Dissolve the dripping in the boiling water. Stir into dry mixture together with the molasses. Boil in a cloth for about 2½ hours.

Makes 6 to 8 servings.

MANX

Manx Pudding

pinch of salt
2 cups all-purpose flour
2 eggs
1 cup milk
2 tablespoons currants

Mix salt and flour. Make a well in the center and add the eggs and milk. Add currants and place in a basin to steam for about 2 hours.
Makes 4 servings.

Binjean

2 cups fresh milk
1 teaspoon "steep"—essence of rennet

Heat milk slightly: stir in steep thoroughly and place in a dish. When cold serve with sugar and cream. A little nutmeg grated on the binjean when cold is also considered to be an improvement!
Makes 4 servings.

Lemon Pudding

1 cup self-rising flour
½ cup brown sugar
½ cup milk
1 large egg (beaten)
juice of 2 lemons
2 tablespoons butter

Mix all the ingredients together. Put in a greased basin and steam for a couple of hours.
Makes 4 servings.

Plum Pudding

2 cups each of all-purpose flour, suet, sugar, brown raisins and
   golden raisins
½ cup blanched almonds
½ cup white breadcrumbs
1 cup mixed peel
pinch of ginger
½ teaspoon baking soda
10 small eggs
2 tablespoons Brandy
½ stick butter, melted

Mix all the above together. Put into greased pudding basins and boil
for 7 - 8 hours. Makes two good sized puddings.

Tynwald Trifle

4 eggs (separate the yolks and whites)
¾ cup granulated sugar
1 tablespoon gelatin
1 cup boiling water
juice and rind of an orange
some orange food coloring

Beat the whites of the eggs until very stiff with the sugar. Add the
gelatin to the water, dissolve. When cooled add the orange juice, rind
and the food coloring. When quite cold, add the mixture to the whites
of egg and the yolks. Beat together until well mixed. When set, spread
with greengage jam and cream.
   Makes 4 servings.

IRISH

Moonshiner's Pudding

3 tablespoons cornstarch
juice of 2 lemons
¾ cup sugar
2 cups boiling water
2 egg whites

Mix cornstarch to a smooth paste with the lemon juice. Add sugar. Slowly pour on the boiling water. Stir well. Boil for 3-4 minutes. Cool, then fold in the stiffly beaten egg whites. Whisk thoroughly. Pour into a wetted mould. Chill and when set turn out onto a dish.

Make a custard with the following:

2 egg yolks
1 teaspoon sugar
vanilla essence
1 cup milk
1 teaspoon cornstarch

Pour the cooled custard around the pudding.
Makes 4 servings.

Irish Currant Tart

2 cups currants
½ cup sugar
½ cup raspberry cordial
3 tablespoons gelatin
1 cooked shortcrust pastry case

Soak the currants overnight in sufficient water to cover them. Add ½ cup sugar and bring to a boil. Add the cordial and thicken with the gelatin. Leave for at least 3 hours. Fill pastry case with the mixture and serve with cream.
Makes 4 servings.

Conemarra Tart

1 cup self-rising flour
½ teaspoon ground ginger
pinch of salt
¼ cup sugar
6 tablespoons butter, divided
¼ cup milk
1 beaten egg
2 large apples

For the top:

½ teaspoon cinnamon
¼ teaspoon nutmeg

Sift flour, ginger, salt and sugar. Rub in half of the butter. Add milk and egg to make a soft dough. Roll out on a floured board. Cover the base of a greased pie dish with the pastry. Grate the apples onto the pastry. Dot with remaining butter. Sprinkle cinnamon and nutmeg over top. Bake in a moderate oven (350 degrees) for 30 minutes. Serve hot with custard.
Makes 4 to 6 servings.

Junket

1 cup light cream
1 cup milk
½ cup granulated sugar
2 teaspoons rennet
mint leaves (to decorate)
pinch of cinnamon and a pinch of sugar to sprinkle over the top

Heat the cream and milk to just warm. Add sugar, dissolve completely. Stir in the rennet. Pour into glasses and leave to set. Sprinkle the tops with the cinnamon/sugar mixture when ready to serve.
Can be served with any of the following stewed fruits: gooseberries, red and black currants or very young pink rhubarb.
Makes 4 servings.

Cork Pudding

6 eggs
1¾ cups granulated sugar
3 cups self-rising flour
1 cup brown sugar
1 stick butter
1½ lb. of black currants, red currants and plums (stoned and
   halved)

An Autumn Pudding as all the fruits were generally available in the garden.

Grease a large 6-cup pie dish. Whisk the eggs and granulated sugar until thick. Add flour and fold.

In a saucepan melt the brown sugar and butter until just bubbling, add the cleaned fruits. Pour this mixture into the pie dish and cover with the flour mixture. Cook in a moderate hot oven (375 degrees) for about 1 to 1½ hours. It should be firm to the touch if cooked. When cooked, turn up-side down and serve with fresh cream.

Makes 6 servings.

SCOTLAND

Scots Black Bun

Fruit Mixture:

   1 cup all-purpose flour
   1 stick butter
   2 cups brown raisins
   4 tablespoons ground almonds
   1 teaspoon cream of tartar
   ¼ cup brown sugar
   2 cups currants
   2 cups golden raisins
   3 eggs, beaten
   pinch each of baking powder, mixed spice, cinnamon, nutmeg,
       pepper and salt
   enough milk to mix

Mix all the dry ingredients together. Add the beaten eggs and milk
to form a dough.

Pastry case:

   1½ sticks butter
   2 cups all-purpose flour
   1 teaspoon lemon juice
   water to mix

Rub the butter into the flour. Add the juice and water to form a stiff
dough. Roll out thinly on a floured board and line a greased 9-inch
square tin with the pastry. Leave sufficient to cover the top. Place the
fruit mixture on top of the pastry and crimp the pastry edges. Bake in
slow oven (275 degrees) for 3-3½ hours.
   Makes 4 to 6 servings.

Tipsy Laird

8 pieces of stale Swiss roll or stale cake
½ cup sherry
raspberry jam
2 tablespoons brandy
2 cups rich custard
1 cup heavy cream
2 drops vanilla essence
juice of 1 lemon and 1 orange

Cut up the Swiss Roll into eight equal pieces. Soak in the sherry. Pour the jam and the brandy (mixed together to thin the jam) over the Swiss roll. Leave to soak for about 5 minutes. Pour cooled custard over. Whip the cream and vanilla essence with lemon and orange juice. Pile on top of the custard. Decorate with glacé cherries and hazelnuts.
Makes 8 servings.

Whiskey Bread Pudding

Put about 8 thick slices of white bread in a large bowl. Add enough warm milk to soak up the bread. To 2 cups raisins add a small cupful of whiskey and 1 cup brown sugar and leave overnight. Beat 3 large eggs and pour over the bread—mash up with a fork, add to the fruit and sprinkle a mixture of 1 tablespoon ginger and 2 tablespoons sugar over the top. Bake in a hot oven (425 degrees) until set and well browned. Leave to cool and cut into slices.
Makes 8 servings.

Boiled Apple Dumplings

6 cooking apples, peeled and cored—cut into halves
sugar (to taste)

For the dumplings:

4 tablespoons butter
1 cup self-rising flour
pinch brown sugar
pinch of cinnamon
1 small beaten egg
milk (if needed to make into a dropping consistency)

Rub butter into flour, sugar, and cinnamon. Mix to a soft dough with the egg and milk. Take a large flat frypan, add the halved apples. Cover with just enough water to cover. Cook until "just" soft. Add spoonfuls of the dough. Cook with a lid on for about 5 minutes. Lift carefully out of the water with a slatted spoon. Serve with cream. Add sugar to taste.
Makes 6 to 8 servings.

Treacle (Molasses) Tart

Shortcrust Pastry—made with:

2 cups flour
1 stick butter
1 egg yolk
pinch of salt

For the filling:

¾ cup light corn syrup
2 tablespoons molasses
1 tablespoon lemon juice
6 tablespoons fine white breadcrumbs
1 teaspoon rum

Line an 8-inch pie dish with the bottom pastry. Leave enough pastry to decorate the top with strips. Mix in together the corn syrup, molasses, lemon juice and breadcrumbs. Add the rum last. Make a lattice top for the pie and bake for 30 minutes in a hot oven (425 degrees). Serve with a custard.

Makes 6 to 8 servings.

WELSH

Snowdon Pudding

¼ cup stoned raisins
½ cup white breadcrumbs
½ cup fine suet
4 tablespoons cornstarch
rind of 3 lemons, grated
¾ cup brown sugar
⅓ cup lemon marmalade
pinch of salt
5 large eggs

Grease a large pudding basin well. Place some of the raisins on the base to decorate. Mix breadcrumbs, suet, cornstarch, lemon rind, brown sugar, marmalade, salt, and remaining raisins together. Beat the eggs and add to the mixture. Pour into the basin and tie securely with a cloth. Boil for 1½-1¾ hours.

Serve with wine sauce:

1¾ glassful (6 oz. size) maderia or sweet sherry
rind of 1 lemon and juice
¼ cup sugar
3 tablespoons butter
1 teaspoon cornstarch

Boil the wine and rind and juice of the lemon and sugar, till, the sugar has dissolved. Remove the rind. Melt the butter, and mix with the cornstarch and wine. Add to the sugar mixture. Boil for one minute. Serve hot poured over the pudding.
Makes 8 servings.

Apple Cake

½ stick butter
¾ cup sugar
2 eggs
2½ cups self-rising flour
¾ cup milk
1 lb. apples, peeled, sliced, and stewed

Cream butter and sugar. Add eggs and beat. Fold in the flour and milk to make a soft dough. Roll out carefully. Cover a big plate with pastry. Spread stewed apples over and place the other half of the pastry on top. Bake in hot oven (425 degrees) for 25 minutes. Eat hot or cold.

Makes 8 servings.

Monmouth Pudding

¼ scant cup hot milk
4 tablespoons sugar (flavored with 4 drops of vanilla essence), divided
2 cups white breadcrumbs
4 small eggs, separated
1 cup chopped dried fruit (soaked in a little sherry overnight)
1 cup strawberry jam
3 tablespoons melted butter

Pour the milk and half of the sugar over the breadcrumbs. Leave to absorb the milk. Separate the yolks and whites of eggs. Whisk whites with the remaining sugar. Pour half the breadcrumb mixture into pudding dish—spread the base of the dish with the sherried soaked fruit (soak overnight for best results). Spread the jam over the bread-crumbs and finish off with the final amoung of bread crumb mixture. Pour melted butter over top. Bake in a slow oven (300 degrees) for 30 minutes or till set. Bring out and pour over whisked whites of eggs. Bake in very hot oven (450 degrees) for 5 minutes until meringue is browned.
Makes 6 servings.

Rhubarb and Apple Crumble

1 lb. rhubarb
1 lb. apples
1 stick butter
2 cups self-rising flour
½ cup sugar
¾ cup porridge oats
½ cup shredded coconut
½ tablespoon cinnamon
½ tablespoon nutmeg

Clean and cook the fruits. Rub butter into flour. Add sugar and the other ingredients. Mix well. Place fruit in a large pie dish. Sprinkle crumble over the top. Bake in a moderate oven (350 degrees) for 30 minutes. Serve hot with fresh cream or custard.

Makes 6 to 8 servings.

Burnt Cream Pudding

1 cup fresh heavy cream
6 small egg yolks
4 tablespoons confectioners' sugar
few drops vanilla essence
¼ cup granulated sugar (for the tops)

Heat cream in a double saucepan. Drop in egg yolks and heat, add confectioners' sugar and vanilla. Cook but do not boil. Stir until the mixture is thickened. Place in a pint sized dish. Leave to cool. Before serving sprinkle the granulated sugar over the top and put under a very hot burner until the top is all "burnt" and browned.

Makes 6 servings.

Breads and Cakes

BRETON

Savarin

¼ cup yeast
½ cup warm water
6 tablespoons sugar, divided
2 sticks butter, melted
8 eggs
1 cup warm milk
4 cups all-purpose flour
1 cup sliced almonds
salt

Savarin Sauce:

2 cups sugar
2 tablespoons orange juice
2 tablespoons lemon juice
2 cups water
¼ cup rum or cointreau

Put all sauce ingredients in a saucepan and bring to a boil. Cool and use as needed.

Mix yeast and water together. Add a very small amount of the sugar. Cream the butter and remaining sugar together and add. Add the eggs one at a time: add the warm milk and flour. Add salt to taste. Leave in a warm place until double in size. (This will take about 2 hours.) Knead. Grease a savarin ring and sprinkle almonds on the base. Pour in yeast batter and set aside again for about an hour. Bake in hot oven (425 degrees) for 30 minutes. Cool.

Make holes in the ring by poking with a skewer. Pour the savarin sauce over and serve with cream. This mixture makes two savarin rings of about a dozen servings each.

Brioche

2 tablespoons yeast
½ cup warm water
2 tablespoons sugar

Mix all ingredients together and allow to stand for 5 minutes. When the yeast has activated, add:

1 teaspoon salt
4 small eggs
1 stick butter, warmed
3½ cups all-purpose flour

Mix until dough is smooth. Leave to prove for about 1½ hours until double in size. Knead again and place in refrigerator in a greased container for 24 hours. Next day, shape into small or a large brioche and cook for about 1 hour for the large and about 20 minutes for the petite brioches.

Cheese Cake

Approx. ½ lb. flaky pastry
3 eggs, separated
1 lb. cream cheese
½ cup sugar
1¼ cup flour
pinch of cinnamon
pinch of salt
3 tablespoons butter, melted
2 oz. plain dark chocolate, grated

Cover the base and sides of a shallow dish with the rolled pastry. Separate the egg yolks and whites. Mix all the ingredients apart from the egg whites, together. Whisk the egg whites and add to the other mixture.

Fill case and cook in a hot oven (425 degrees). When cooked sprinkle with some sugar and a little more of the grated chocolate.

Makes 6 to 8 servings.

Vanilla Cake

8 cups all-purpose flour
6 sticks butter
1 teaspoon vanilla essence
2½ cups sugar
2 eggs
1 cup blanched almonds

Work all the ingredients to a firm dough. Make into small rounds and bake in a hot oven (425 degrees) until brown.

Sugar Biscuits

1 stick unsalted butter
½ cup granulated sugar
2 cups all-purpose flour
pinch of salt
½ teaspoon baking powder
pinch each of cinnamon, cloves and nutmeg
1 large well beaten egg
¼ cup extra sugar (for the tops)

Rub in the butter into the sugar and flour. Add the salt, baking powder, and spices. Add egg and mix to a softish dough. Roll out on a floured board to about $1/8$-inch thickness. Place on non-stick trays and dust with extra sugar. Bake for 30 minutes in a hot oven (425 degrees).

Ginger Cakes

1 stick butter
½ cup brown sugar
½ cup light corn syrup
2 cups self-rising flour
good pinch baking soda
3 teaspoons finely ground ginger

Melt in a large saucepan the butter, sugar and corn syrup. Cool. Add the dry ingredients and mix well. Roll small balls between your palms and flatten onto a greased baking sheet. Bake in a hot oven (425 degrees) for 15–20 minutes.

When cool these cookies become quite hard and should be kept in an airtight tin.

Makes 8 servings.

CORNISH

Dorset Knobs

1 tablespoon sugar
1 tablespoon yeast
2 tablespoons butter
1 cup warm milk
pinch of salt
4 cups all-purpose flour

Cream the sugar and yeast. Add the melted butter to the milk and add everything to the flour. Knead to a smooth dough. Form into small rolls and leave to prove for 1 hour in a warm spot. Bake in a hot oven (425 degrees) for 20 minutes.
Makes 8 servings.

Drop Scones

½ stick butter
2 cups self-rising flour
1 egg (beaten)
½ cup milk
pinch of salt
2 tablespoons sugar

Rub butter into flour. Add other ingredients and mix to a soft dough. Roll on floured board. Cut into rounds. Bake in a hot oven (425 degrees) for 12-15 minutes or until golden brown.
Makes 8 servings.

Redruth Tea Cake

Overnight soak 1 cup cold tea: 1 lb. dried mixed fruit: 1 cup brown sugar. Next day add 2 cups self-rising flour: 1 well beaten egg and pinch of salt. Mix well. Pour into greased loaf tin and bake in moderate oven (350 degrees) for 1½ hours. Leave one whole day before cutting.

Wholewheat Bread

1 tablespoon yeast
1 tablespoon sugar
1 tablespoon light corn syrup
1½ cups warm milk
2 cups wholewheat flour
pinch salt

Cream the yeast and sugar. Add the syrup and milk. Make a well in the center of the flour and pour in the liquid. Add salt and knead. Let prove for about an hour in a warm place. Punch down and form ino round loaves. Leave to rise again for 30 minutes. Bake in a hot oven (425 degrees) for 40 minutes to 1 hour.
Makes 8 to 12 servings.

Saffron Bread

1 envelope active dry yeast
1 cup warm milk (steep in the hot water for 5 - 10 minutes)
½ stick butter
6 tablespoons sugar
4 cups all-purpose flour
pinch of salt
2 to 3 tablespoons hot water
small teaspoon of saffron threads

Prove the yeast in the warm milk. Add the warmed butter. Add sugar. Add the flour and pinch salt and mix well. Knead for a few minutes. Leave to prove for 2 hours. Re-knead with additional water and saffron threads and place into 2 lb. loaf tins. Leave to rise for 30 minutes. Bake in a hot oven (425 degrees) for 30–40 minutes. Cool on a wire tray.
Makes 8 to 12 servings.

Rum Tart

6 oz. rich short crust pastry
1 cup fine breadcrumbs
juice of 1 lemon
pinch of salt
6 tablespoons black molasses
2 tablespoons rum
2 tablespoons shredded coconut

Line a pie plate with the pastry and prick base. Mix other ingredients together. Fill the pastry case and bake in moderate to hot oven (375 degrees) for about 20-25 minutes. Serve with cream.
Makes 8 servings.

Almond and Ginger Cakes

½ cup fine brown sugar
1½ sticks butter
2 egg yolks
3 teaspoons light corn syrup
juice of an orange
2 cups self-rising flour
good pinch ginger
½ cup chopped almonds

Cream sugar and butter together. Add egg yolks. Add the syrup and orange juice. Mix well with flour and ginger. Form into small balls, flatten and sprinkle on the chopped almonds. Bake in low slow oven (275 degrees) until well cooked.
Makes 10 servings.

Booty Cake

This cake could well have been made with the spoils of the smugglers that were around the Cornish Coves in the old times.

Soak

¼ lb. green cherries
½ lb. pineapple
½ lb. dessert dates
¼ lb. glacé apricots

in

½ cup rum or brandy

Leave overnight if possible.

To the above add:

½ cup brown sugar creamed in 6 tablespoons butter
2 beaten eggs
½ cup all-purpose flour
½ teaspoon baking powder
1 teaspoon vanilla essence
1 teaspoon brandy
pinch of salt

Place in a greased cake tin and bake in moderate oven (350 degrees) for approximately 1-1½ hours or until cooked. Leave for one whole day before cutting.

Makes 8 to 12 servings.

St. Ives Cake

1 tablespoon yeast
1 cup white sugar
4 sticks butter
8 cups flour
2 cups currants
pinch salt
½ teaspoon saffron
½ teaspoon nutmeg
2½ cups warm water
¼ cup chopped peel

Mix yeast and some of the sugar to a cream. Rub the butter and flour to fine bread crumb mixture. Add all other ingredients. Leave to rise in warm place to double in size. Punch down. Put into greased loaf or cake tins and let rise again. Bake in moderate oven (350 degrees) for 1-1¼ hours. Cool on rack.

Makes 8 to 12 servings.

Gingerbread Cake

1 stick butter
1 cup brown sugar
1 tablespoon molasses
2 eggs
1 teacup milk
½ cup currants
2 cups self-rising flour
1 teaspoon mixed spice
½ teaspoon ginger
pinch salt

Cream butter and sugar. Add molasses. Add the eggs and milk, then fruit and flour. Add mixed spice, ginger, and salt. Bake in moderate oven (350 degrees) for 45 minutes. Sprinkle the top with sugar.

Makes 8 servings.

MANX

Fruit Bonnag

2 tablespoons lard
4 cups self-rising flour
handful currants, golden raisins, mixed peel and brown raisins
¼ cup sugar
milk to mix
2 tablespoons butter

Rub fat into flour. Mix in fruit and sugar. Add milk and butter to make a soft dough. Cook in a flat meat tin in a moderate oven (350 degrees) until browned and cooked.
Makes 8 to 12 servings.

Bunloaf

2½ cups all-purpose flour
pinch of salt
6 tablespoons lard
6 tablespoons butter
½ teaspoon mixed spice
½ teaspoon nutmeg
½ teaspoon baking soda
⅔ cup brown sugar
4 tablespoons mixed peel
1 level teaspoon black molasses
2 eggs
4 tablespoons buttermilk
1 cup currants
1 cup golden raisins
¼ cup brown raisins

Place flour and salt in a bowl. Add lard and butter and rub in well. Stir in mixed spice, nutmeg, baking soda, sugar and peel. Add molasses

to eggs and buttermilk and beat well. Add to dry ingredients and add currants and raisins. Place in a greased loaf tin and bake in a moderate oven (350 degrees) for 2½ hours. Leave to cool in the tin.
Makes 8 to 10 servings.

Manx Buttermilk Scones

4 cups flour
1 tablespoon baking soda
½ tablespoon cream of tartar
pinch of salt
pinch of black pepper
½ stick slightly melted butter
enough buttermilk to make into a soft dough

Place flour, baking soda, cream of tartar, salt and pepper into a bowl. Pour in butter and buttermilk. Mix to a soft dough. Cut into round shape and bake in a very hot oven (450 degrees) until browned. Eat with cheese whilst warm.
Makes 10 to 12 servings.

Soda Cakes

1 stick butter
8 cups flour
1 teaspoon salt
1 teaspoon baking soda
buttermilk

Mix the butter and flour to resemble fine breadcrumbs. Add the salt, baking soda and buttermilk to form a soft dough. Roll out to ¼-inch thickness and trim the edges to the shape required. Bake on a griddle over a slow fire. Brown both sides.
Makes 12 servings.

Tynwald Cake

2 sticks butter
1¼ cups granulated sugar
6 eggs
1½ cups flour
½ cup ground rice flour
1½ teaspoons ground ginger
1½ teaspoons baking powder
1½ teaspoons vanilla essence
few drops cochineal
shredded coconut (for sprinkling)
chocolate icing
2 tablespoons pistachio nuts, chopped
cream filling

Line 3 round cake tins (8", 6", 4") with greased paper. Cream butter and sugar: add eggs one at a time. Add some flour with each egg. Mix flour, rice flour, ginger and baking powder. Stir lightly. Add essence and if needed, a little milk. Color a delicate pink. Spread mixture over base of tins. Sprinkle tops with coconut and bake in moderate oven (350 degrees) for 30 minutes. When cold cover with chocolate icing. Place one cake on top of another, large at the base. Sprinkle with the chopped pistachio nuts. Place a small flag on top with the Manx coat of arms. Serve with cream filling.

Cream filling:

½ cup sugar
1 stick unsalted butter
2 tablespoons glacé cherries
1 teaspoon vanilla essence

Cream sugar and butter. Add cherries and vanilla essence and mix.

Chocolate Icing:

   small piece of lard
   4 tablespoons grated chocolate
   1 cup confectioners' sugar
   2-3 tablespoons hot water
   vanilla essence

Melt lard and chocolate. Mix in confectioners' sugar. Add hot water. Add vanilla essence. Use at once.
   Makes 12 to 15 servings.

IRISH

Irish Soda Bread

4 cups all-purpose flour
pinch of salt
1 teaspoon cream of tartar
1 teaspoon baking soda
1 stick butter
½ cup sugar
1 cup golden raisins
4 tablespoons chopped peel
1 cup (generous) sour milk

Sieve flour, salt, cream of tartar, and baking soda together. Rub in butter until like fine breadcrumbs. Stir in sugar, raisins, and peel. Add the milk and mix to a soft dough. Knead slightly. Place in a greased loaf tin and bake in a hot oven (425 degrees) for 1 hour, turn down heat to moderate and bake for further 30 minutes. Cool before cutting. Slice and butter.
Makes 1 large loaf.

Golden Raisin and Molasses Bread

½ cup boiling water
1 tablespoon molasses
½ tablespoon fresh yeast
½ tablespoon sugar
2 tablespoons butter
2 cups wholewheat flour
pinch of salt
4 tablespoons golden raisins
2 tablespoons candied peel

Place the water and molasses in a large bowl. Cream the yeast and sugar with the butter. Add the yeast mixture to the water and molasses.

Add the flour, salt, raisins, and peel. Knead well. Allow to rise for 1 hour. Knock down again, and leave to rise again in a greased loaf tin for 30 minutes. Brush top with milk and sugar. Bake in hot oven (425 degrees) for 30 minutes.

Makes 1 large loaf.

Home Made Bread

½ lb. potatoes
15 cups all-purpose flour
pinch of salt
warm water to mix
2 cups home made yeast

Home made yeast can be made as follows:

1 small handful hops
6 cups water
3 tablespoons sugar
1 tablespoon salt
1 tablespoon flour
2 large potatoes

Boil hops in the water for 1 hour. Strain. Mix sugar, salt and flour. Pour half of the hot liquid onto the sugar mixture. Stir well. Grate potatoes, pour remaining liquid over the potatoes and stir until it becomes like the consistency of thick cream. Add the two mixtures together and keep in bottles—only half fill bottles. Cork and leave for about 3-4 days before using.

For the bread:
Cook potatoes and put through a sieve. Sift flour and add salt, the potatoes, enough water to make a smooth dough, and the yeast. Cover and leave overnight in a warm spot. Next day divide into three loaves and knead again. Place in greased loaf tins and place to rise again for 30 minutes. Bake in hot oven (425 degrees) for 1 hour. Cool on wire rack.

Makes 3 loaves.

Apple and Potato Cake

1 teaspoon melted butter
1 cup sugar
1 well beaten egg
½ cup golden raisins
¾ cup milk
2 drops lemon essence
2 cups self-rising flour
1 teaspoon nutmeg
¼ cup mashed cooked apple
¼ cup mashed cooked potatoes

Beat the butter into the apple and potato mixture. Add the rest of the ingredients. Place in a greased cake tin. Sprinkle over the top the following topping:

1 cup all-purpose flour
¼ cup melted butter
1 cup brown sugar
pinch cinnamon

Mix all well together. Bake in a moderate oven (350 degrees) for 40 minutes. Leave to cool in the tin.

Makes 8 to 10 servings.

Whisky Cake

½ cup chopped almonds (reserve a few for the top)
2 tablespoons whisky
1½ sticks butter
⅔ cup brown sugar
3 eggs, beaten
2 cups self-rising flour
1 teaspoon baking powder
pinch of salt
¼ lb. cherries (pitted and quartered)

Soak the almonds in the whisky for about an hour. Cream butter and sugar. Add the beaten eggs, nuts and whisky, flour, baking powder, salt, and cherries. Bake in moderate oven (350 degrees) for 45 minutes.
Makes 8 to 10 servings.

Lardy Cake

2 lbs. warm risen bread dough
1¼ cups lard
1⅔ cups brown sugar
1 cup currants

Flatten the dough to an oblong. Cut up lard to small pieces. Place on top of dough. Sprinkle with the sugar and currants. Bake in fairly hot oven (400 degrees) for approx. 1¼ hours.
Makes 8 to 10 servings.

Irish Cheese Cake

½ lb. rich shortcrust pastry

Filling:

1 lb. cream cheese (Quark or similar)
$2/3$ cup granulated sugar
3 small well beaten eggs
1 cup sour cream
1 tablespoon lemon juice
few drops of vanilla essence

Put into a bowl the cheese, sugar, eggs and mix. Add sour cream, beat until well aired. Add lemon juice and vanilla essence and stir in. Makes 6 to 8 servings.

SCOTLAND

Babs

1 tablespoon yeast
1 tablespoon sugar
4 tablespoons melted butter
1 cup warm milk
4 cups all-purpose flour
1 teaspoon salt
1 egg, beaten

Mix the yeast and sugar until liquid. Pour melted butter into yeast mixture. Add warmed milk. Combine flour and salt. Make a well in the flour mixture and add the yeast mixture and the well beaten egg. Allow to prove until double in size. Cut up into small pieces and shape. Allow to prove again for about an hour. Bake in hot oven (425 degrees) for about 15-20 minutes.
Makes 8 to 12 servings.

Oatcakes

2 cups fine oatmeal
pinch of salt
pinch of baking soda
1 tablespoon beef dripping
1 cup hot water

Mix dry ingredients together. Rub in the dripping. Mix with the water to a pastry dough consistency. Roll out on a floured board. Cut into squares and cook on a hot griddle.
Makes 8 to 10 cakes.

Scottish Bannock

This is almost like a fruit cake and was reputed to be one of Queen Victoria's favourite tea-time treats.

2 tablespoons yeast
2 tablespoons sugar
½ cup brown sugar
2½ cups warmed milk, divided
½ cup melted butter
8 cups all-purpose flour
pinch of salt
½ cup golden raisins
½ cup candied peel
½ cup hazelnuts/walnuts, chopped
few almonds for decoration

Mix the yeast and sugars until a liquid. Add half the warmed milk. Add the melted butter. Sift the flour and salt and mix in the raisins, peel, and hazelnuts. Add the yeast mixture and the rest of the milk to the flour and fruit mixture. Leave in a warm place to double in size. Knead well and put into a large round tin which has been well greased. Sprinkle almonds over the top of cake. Bake in moderate oven (350 degrees) for about 45-50 minutes. Leave for 1 day before cutting. Slice and spread with butter.
Makes 8 to 12 servings.

Clootie Dumplings

4 cups self-rising flour
½ teaspoon salt
¾ cup golden raisins
½ teaspoon cinnamon
½ cup sugar
1 cup currants
¾ cup brown raisins
½ teaspoon mixed spice
¼ lb. suet
1 tablespoon molasses
milk

Mix flour, salt, golden raisins, cinnamon, sugar, currants, brown raisins, mixed spice, and suet together. Stir in the molasses and enough milk to make a stiff dough. Place in a clean scalded cloth loosely (this pudding swells). Place in boiling water and cook for 3½-4 hours. Pull off cloth. Serve hot with custard as a pudding, or cold like a cake.
Makes 8 servings.

Shortbread

3 sticks butter
1²/₃ cups sugar
2½ cups plain flour
2½ cups ground rice
pinch of salt
2 eggs
2 tablespoons light cream

Rub the butter into the sugar, flour, rice, and salt. Beat the eggs and the cream together. Add to the mixture and knead until it is fine. Roll out to ⅛-inch thickness on a well greased board. Cut into fingers or bake in a mould. Prick with a fork before baking in a moderate oven (350 degrees) until light gold color. Cool.
Makes 8 servings.

Dundee Cake

10 tablespoons butter
$^2/_3$ cup brown sugar
3 beaten eggs
1¼ cups flour
½ cup currants
½ cup cherries and raisins (mixed)
½ cup golden raisins
$^1/_3$ cup mixed peel
¼ teaspoon nutmeg
¼ teaspoon mixed spice
pinch of salt
½ teaspoon baking powder
¼ cup almonds (for the top), slivered

Cream the butter and sugar. Add the beaten eggs and flour. Add the fruit and the peel. Gradually add the spices, salt and baking powder. Place in a greased tin and put the almonds on the top in a circular shape. Bake in a moderate oven (350 degrees) for 2½ hours or until middle is firm. Cool on tray and store for two days before cutting.

Makes 6 to 8 servings.

Scottish Beer Cake

1 cup softened butter
1¾ cups brown sugar
4 eggs
3 cups self-rising flour
2 teaspoons baking powder
¾ cup beer
1 cup chopped almonds
1 cup chopped walnuts

Cream butter and sugar. Add eggs and flour alternately. Add baking powder. Add beer and then nuts. Decorate top of cake with a few of the nuts. Bake in a moderate oven (350 degrees) for 1 hour. Cool and leave for one day before eating.

Makes 6 to 8 servings.

WALES

Bara Cymraeg

2 tablespoons yeast
2 tablespoons sugar
2 tablespoons butter
4 cups warm water
8 cups white flour
4 cups brown flour
1 tablespoon salt

Mix yeast and sugar. Add the butter to the warm water. Mix flours and salt in a large bowl. Add the yeast, sugar and water to the flour. Mix to a dough. Grease the bread tins. Half fill the tins. Leave to prove in warm place. Bake in hot oven (400 degrees) for 35-40 minutes.
Makes 10 to 12 servings.

Bara Brith (made with yeast)

1 tablespoon yeast
½ cup sugar
1 cup milk and water
4 cups all-purpose flour
1 teaspoon mixed spice
pinch salt
½ stick butter
1 egg
½ cup golden raisins
½ cup currants
½ cup candied peel
2 tablespoons stoned raisins

Cream yeast and sugar. Heat the milk/water mixture to luke warm, mix in with the yeast. Mix flour, spice and salt. Make a well in the center and pour in the yeast mixture. Stir. Cover with a cloth and leave in a warm place to prove for 30 minutes. Melt the butter. Add to the gently proving yeast mixture. Sprinkle with some extra flour. Leave for another half hour. Beat the egg and add to the dough. Knead well, stir in the fruit. Turn mixture onto floured board. Grease 2 lb. loaf tin. Place mixture in tins (makes enough for two tins). Leave to prove again for 30 minutes. Bake in hot oven (400 degrees) for 15 minutes. Turn heat down to moderate and cook for another 35 minutes. Cool on a wire tray. Leave for one day before eating. Slice and butter.

Makes 2 loaves.

Bara Brith (without yeast)

8 cups self-rising flour
2 lbs. mixed dried fruit
4 tablespoons marmalade
2 eggs
12 tablespoons sugar
2 tablespoons ground mixed spice
2 cups warm tea (strained)
honey for glazing

Mix flour and dried fruit. Add marmalade, beaten eggs, sugar and spice to the warm tea. Add the liquid to the dry mixture and mix well. Line and grease 4 loaf tins. Place mixture into the tins. Glaze with honey. Bake in a moderate oven (350 degrees) for 1½ hours. Cool on wire racks. Store for one day before cutting.

Makes 4 loaves.

Bara Ceirch

These are similar to the Scottish oatcakes but they are thinner.

2 tablespoons butter
2 tablespoons lard
¾ cup warm water (Boil the water and leave to cool for 5 minutes.)
pinch of salt
1 tablespoon sugar
2 cups fine oatmeal

Add the butter and lard to the water. Mix in the salt, sugar and oatmeal. Make into a soft dough. Sprinkle oatmeal on a board and flatten with the palm of the hands. Place onto a hot bakestone or a "llechfaen" as it is called in Cardiganshire, to harden. Bake the oatcakes for about 5-7 minutes on each side on a griddle. These oatcakes are not the easiest to make, but well worth mastering. Keep in an airtight tin.
Makes 6 servings.

Crempog

1 teaspoon baking soda
2 teaspoons cream of tartar
pinch of salt
¾ cup self-rising flour
4 eggs
1 cup milk
4 tablespoons buttermilk
butter for frying
¼ cup sugar

Add the baking soda, salt, and cream of tartar to the flour. Beat eggs. Add the eggs to the milk and buttermilk. Make a well in the flour. Mix the flour and liquid together. Heat butter in a cast iron fry pan. Spoon mixture into pan and cook till golden on both sides. Serve warm, buttered and sprinkled with sugar. Honey is also good on Crempog.
Makes 8 servings.

Breads and Cakes

Welsh Yeast Cake

1 lb. golden raisins, currants, mixed peel, and a few cherries
   (mixed)
½ lb. brown raisins
1¼ cups cold tea
½ tablespoon yeast
1 cup soft brown sugar
4 cups all-purpose flour
pinch of salt
¼ teaspoon each of cinnamon, nutmeg and mixed spice
2 beaten eggs

Soak the fruit in the tea for about 4-6 hours. Mix the yeast and sugar to a cream, and add to the flour, salt, and spices. Add the fruit and tea. Add beaten eggs. Leave to prove for about 45 minutes in a warm place. Bake in a slow to moderate oven (325 degrees) for about 1-1½ hours. This will make a good sized cake. Leave for one day before cutting.
   Makes 12 servings.

Cacen Gneifio

1 cup sugar
2 sticks butter
2 eggs
2 cups self-rising flour
pinch of salt
½ cup almonds (slivered)
½ lb. currants
½ lb. golden raisins
½ cup candied peel
½ cup sherry or port
1½ teaspoons mixed spice

Cream the sugar and butter. Add the eggs to the mixture with a little flour to stop the mixture from curdling. Sift the flour and salt. Add the nuts and fruit and peel to the sifted flour. Add sherry and mixed spice and stir well into the mixture. Place into a greased baking tin and bake for approximately 1-2 hours in a moderate oven (350 degrees). Before baking sprinkle the top with nuts.

Makes 8 to 10 servings.

Cage Bach

pinch of salt
4 cups self-rising flour
2½ sticks butter
2 eggs
3 tablespoons milk
¾ cup sugar
1 cup mixed fruit

Sift the salt and flour. Rub in the butter till it resembles fine breadcrumbs. Beat the eggs and milk and add to the dry mixture. Add sugar and mixed fruit and make a stiff dough. Roll out onto a floured board. Cut into small rounds. Cook on a griddle for about 3 minutes.

This mixture will make about three dozen cakes, which will keep for about a fortnight in an airtight tin.

Teisen Lap (Plate Cake)

2 sticks butter
4 cups self-rising flour
pinch of nutmeg
½ cup sugar
1 cup mixed fruit (currants, golden raisins, and brown raisins)
2 eggs
1 cup buttermilk

Rub the butter into the flour. Add the nutmeg, sugar, and mixed fruit. Beat the eggs well and add to the milk. Add the liquid to the dry mixture to make a soft dough. Grease a shallow dish and bake in a moderate oven (350 degrees) for about 30 minutes. These cakes are made and eaten all over Wales. Teisen means 'tart' or 'cake'—Lap, a 'plate'.

Makes 8 to 12 servings.

Teisen Galan Gaeaf

2 sticks butter
1 cup sugar
4 eggs
3 cups all-purpose flour
pinch of salt
1 teaspoon baking powder
1¼ lbs. mixed fruit (1 lb. fruit-¼ lb. nuts, blanched almonds and
   walnuts)

Cream butter and sugar. Add eggs, one at a time, and beat till fluffy.
Add the sifted flour and salt and baking powder. Fold in, and lastly,
fold in the fruit and nuts. Bake in a lined and greased cake tin in a slow
to moderate oven (325 degrees) for about 2 hours. This cake may be
iced if desired.
Makes 10 servings.

Huish Cake

2 sticks butter
2½ cups granulated sugar
8 eggs
1½ cups flour
1½ cups ground rice
caraway seeds

Cream butter and sugar. Separate eggs. Beat yolks into butter and
sugar mixture. Add flour and rice. Whisk egg whites until stiff. Add to
the mixture and stir well with a steel spoon. Add caraway seeds. Grease
two 7" tins and bake in moderate oven (350 degrees) for 1¼ hours.
This cake was served at a baby's christening ceremony, or sometimes
for "high tea" on Sundays.
Makes 10 servings.

Tarten Llysiau Duon Bach

8 oz. (½ pound) short crust pastry

Prepare the pastry and line a shallow baking tin with it. Prick the base and blind bake for 20 minutes.

1 lb. berries
½ cup sugar
1½ teaspoons gelatin
½ cup water
1 cup fresh cream

Clean and wash the berries and cook till soft. Cool. Add the sugar and dissolve the gelatin in the water. Pour gelatin over fruit and pour into pastry case. Whip cream and decorate the top of the tart with the cream.

Llysiau Duon Bach are very like Bilberries and as children we used to eat them from the hedges on our way home from school in the summer.

Makes 8 servings.

Tymplen Ceirch (Dumplings)

4 cups fine oatmeal
1 stick butter
1¼ cups self-rising flour
½ cup currants
pinch of salt
1½ cups of buttermilk

Mix oatmeal, butter, flour, currants, and salt together. Add enough milk to make into a fine dough. Roll into small balls in floured hands. Cook very gently in boiling water for about 40-50 minutes. Drain and serve hot. These dumplings are a very old and traditional dish of Wales and can be served with cawl, ham, or as a sweet pudding with warm custard.

Makes 8 servings.

Bara Lawr (Laverbread)

1 lb. prepared laverbread
½ cup oatmeal
½ stick butter
little lemon juice

The seaweed needs to be boiled for six hours or so, or until it is soft. When soft, cut into servable pieces and coat with the oatmeal. Fry the pieces in the hot butter for about 5-10 minutes. Eat hot. Sprinkle with a little lemon juice. Laverbread is sold in the fish markets of Wales and it should be eaten as fresh as possible. It is therefore not a good idea to buy laverbread in bulk!

Makes 6 servings.

Drinks

CORNISH

Punch

pinch of nutmeg, cinnamon and cloves
½ cup sugar
2½ bottles iced water or soda water
1 bottle rum
juice of 6 lemons
1 bottle brandy

Place the spices and sugar with the water in a pan. Boil for 5 minutes. Strain when cold, add rum and brandy.

Ginger Beer

1 gallon water
juice of 2 lemons
2½ cups sugar
2 tablespoons ginger
4 tablespoons cream of tartar
1 tablespoon yeast

Place water in a large saucepan: add the lemon juice, sugar, ginger, and cream of tartar. Bring to a boil and leave to get lukewarm. When still luke warm add the yeast and leave in a warm place for 24 hours. Strain and bottle. Use in about four days.

MANX

Beetroot Wine

6 lbs. old beetroot
4-5 quarts water
10 cups sugar
2 oranges (juice and peel)
2 lemons (juice and peel)
¼ cup lime juice
2 tablespoons fresh yeast

Cook the beetroot in water. When cooked, peel and chop up into small pieces. Pour the water into a large stew pan and add the beetroot, sugar, and the juices and peels of the citrus fruits. Add the lime juice. Bring slowly to the boil and boil for about 5-10 mins. Cool to lukewarm and add the yeast. Allow to ferment in an earthenware jar or crock for at least a week. Stir well each day. Strain, bottle and keep in a dark place for at least six months—longer if possible .

Potato Wine

½ lb. potatoes
3 pieces ginger
1 gallon cold water
2 lemons (juice)
2 oranges (juice)
8 cups sugar

Place the peeled and cut potatoes, ginger and water into a large pan. Boil for 15 minutes. When cool strain the potato water onto the juices of the lemons, oranges and sugar. Boil for another 45 minutes very slowly. Allow to get cold. When quite cold bottle in clean bottles and when the wine has stopped fermenting cork well. Keep in a dark place for 3-4 months.

IRISH

Irish Coffee

Heat an Irish coffee tankard. Pour one jigger of Irish whisky into the tankard. Add 3 cubes of sugar and top with black coffee to within an inch of the top. Stir to dissolve coffee. Add whipped cream. Do not stir after cream has been added.

This recipe was given to me by a Dublin lass and this little ditty came with it:
Coffee rich as an Irish brogue
Coffee strong as friendly hands,
Sugar sweet as a tongue of a rogue
Whisky smooth as the wit of the bard.

The Toast—Slainte (Good Health)

Irish Punch

Combine in a large punch bowl, 2 quarts sweet cider, ½ bottle vodka, ¼ bottle Irish whisky, and ¼ bottle sweet sherry. Slice 3 oranges and 2 lemons and add these together with ¼ cup sugar. Chop some mint, add and chill. Lastly add a syphon of soda and ice cubes. Makes about 20 helpings.

SCOTLAND

Hot Toddy

2 tablespoons honey
¼ cup boiling water
¼ teaspoon lemon juice
¼ cup whisky

Melt the honey in the boiling water. Add the lemon juice and whisky. Drink whilst hot.

A toddy was traditionally stirred with a silver spoon and served in a crystal glass. An earthenware mug does not, however, crack so easily.

Athol Brose

2½ cups honey
1 cup cold water
2½ cups whisky

Place honey in a large pan. Add water. Heat until honey is dissolved. Add whisky when cooled. Stir until it becomes frothy. Bottle and cork.

Rowanberry Liqueur

1 cup rowanberries
2 cups brandy
syrup (2 cups cold water and 5 cups sugar)

Leave the berries on a shelf until dried and shrivelled. Place the berries in the brandy and leave for at least a week. Strain and mix with the syrup. Bottle and cork. The berries are picked around September and the liqueur should not be drunk before Christmas time.

WALES

Medd (Mead)

¼ cup yeast
small piece of bread
2 gallons water
8 cups honey
5 cups white sugar
4 lemons (juice)
2 tablespoons cloves
piece of ginger (scoured)

Spread the yeast on a piece of bread. Boil the water, honey, and sugar. Stand in an earthenware pot. Skim off any scum. Add lemon juice, cloves and ginger. Leave to cool. When just warm float the bread and yeast on the top. Cover with a clean cloth. Leave for about 6-8 days. Strain and bottle. Corks should be loose to start with. Leave for at least 5-6 months.

Diod Fain

There are numerous ways of making this Welsh wine, but this is just one recipe:

4 large lemons
5 cups white sugar
3 oz. stem ginger root
2 gallons boiling water
¼ cup fresh yeast

Squeeze the lemons and grate a little of the peel away. Pour the juice over the sugar. Bruise the ginger and place in a pan. Pour over the boiling water and leave to cool. When nearly cold add the yeast and leave to stand for a whole day. Bottle between 24-36 hours. Leave for 1 week and then it is ready to drink.

Barm

2 good handfuls of hops (tied into a muslin bag)
2 quarts cold water
1 handful of salt
1 handful of sugar
3 boiled potatoes (peeled)

Put all the above into a large bowl or bucket. Warm on the stove until blood warm. Leave overnight to ferment. Skim and bottle. Drink in about a week's time.

Tea Wine

3 lemons
5 cups brown sugar
2 tablespoons yeast
¾ lb. raisins
8 cups tea

Put lemon (cut into segments), sugar, yeast, and raisins into the tea. Keep warm to let it ferment. About a week will be enough. Strain and bottle.

Metheglin

3 oz. whole ginger
1 gallon warm water
7 cups honey
2 tablespoons yeast

Bruise the ginger. Pour water onto the honey (a large bucket). Add the ginger. Boil for 2-3 hours. Cool. Cover and stand in a warm place for a week. Test for sweetness. (If you put an egg into the mixture—an egg with the shell still intact—it will rise to the top of the mixture if sweet enough. If not and the egg sinks, add more honey.) Add the yeast, stir well and put back on the fire to warm. Do not boil. Cool and when cold, bottle and cork tightly.

Other Recipes

BRETON

Lemon Butter

4 sticks butter
2½ cups granulated sugar
1 cup lemon juice
8 eggs (well beaten)

Place all ingredients in a double boiler. Cook for approximately 20 minutes. Use for sandwich cake fillings and tartlets. Keeps well.

Mayonnaise

3 egg yolks
½ teaspoon lemon juice
½ teaspoon vinegar
½ teaspoon salt
1½ cups olive oil
pinch of black pepper

Whip the egg yolks. Add lemon juice, vinegar and salt. Add oil, drop by drop and beat well. Add pepper. Keep in an airtight container.

IRISH

Baked Potatoes

Wash and scrub the potatoes and place amongst the hot ashes under the fire. Leave until soft. Split in half and eat with butter and black pepper.

Red Currant Jelly

6 lbs. red currants
3 cups sugar

Wash and clean the currants. Place into a large pan and add just enough water to cover the base of the pan. Simmer gently for about ¾-1 hour. When cooked, leave to strain through a muslin bag. Measure the juice and add 3 cups sugar to each 2 cups of juice. Bring to the boil for 2 minutes. Cool slightly and bottle into warmed jars.

SCOTLAND

Porridge

²/₃ cup oatmeal
2½ cups cold water
pinch of salt

Combine all ingredients and heat to thick consistency. In Scotland the porridge is always stirred with a spurtle. I do not know if the porridge tasted better when the spurtle was used but I was told by an old Scottish friend that porridge not stirred with a spurtle is not porridge!

Tablet

2½ cups sugar
1 tablespoon glucose sugar
1 gill water
1 stick butter
½ teaspoon vinegar
¼ cup almonds

Put the sugar and glucose into the water and heat until dissolved. Boil gently for ten minutes. Add the butter and vinegar. Cook until it will set when a drop is placed in cold water. Add the almonds just before taking off the heat.

WALES

Cyflaith

1 cup brown sugar
¾ cup light corn syrup
1½ sticks butter
few drops of vinegar

Place all ingredients into a large saucepan and boil together for about ten minutes, or until the mixture forms a soft ball when a drop is placed in cold water. When ready pour into a greased flat tin. Cut into squares when cool and store in an airtight tin. This was often made for the "calennig children" who called to wish the family a Happy New Year on the first day of the year.

Shincyn

1 cup milk
1 slice thick buttered toast
1 tablespoon sugar
drop of tea

Boil the milk. Cut bread into cubes. Add sugar and a little tea—just to add color. Pour over milk. This was a supper dish in West Wales but how it got the name "Shincyn" has remained a mystery.

Welsh Rarebit

4 slices of toast
½ lb. sharp cheese (grated)
4 tablespoons brown ale
4 tablespoons butter
salt and pepper
pinch of mustard

Put the ale into a saucepan and add the cheese. Melt very slowly. Add the seasonings and butter. Toast and butter the bread. When mixture is very hot pour over the toast and grill until browned. Serve at once.

Bara Llaeth

Into a basin put some small cubes of buttered bread (white). Add sugar to taste and pour on boiling milk. Leave for a few minutes and when cooled, eat. An old supper dish in Wales.

Llymrv

To 2 lbs. oatmeal, add enough buttermilk and water to make a runny consistency. Leave for a couple of days to stand. Pour the mixture through a fine sieve. Simmer for about an hour and stir all the while. Serve with salt and sweet warmed milk.

Dippy

Boil about 1 pound potatoes and about ½ pound pilchards in light cream. Cook and then cool slightly and eat with fresh bread.

Hobbins

Some suet, lard and enough flour to make fine breadcrumbs. Mix with milk to a stiff paste. Roll out to ½-inch thickness and some 4-inch squares. Fill with figs and parcel up. Cook for 30 minutes in a hot oven (425 degrees).

Gruel

Steep some oatmeal in water for several hours. Stir and strain. Put into a pan and cover with half a ping of water. Boil for about one hour. Add some slat and pepper and a spoonful of honey and butter. A Scottish "pick me up."

Cottage Jowdle

Cut up enough potatoes, rutabagas, carrots and green cabbage to fill a stewpot. Add some dripping, fry until browned. Add some water and 3 chopped onions. Cover and cook until soft. Season to taste. An old Cornish supper dish.

Scottish Candy

12 tablespoons sugar
6 tablespoons light corn syrup (molasses if you want them to be more bitter)
3 tablespoons baking soda

Boil the sugar and syrup (molasses). Stir all the time. Boil for about 10-15 minutes. Take from heat and stir in the baking soda. Stir well and pour into a greased flat tin. Break into squares when cold.

Index

Index

Index

Also from Hippocrene . . .

TRADITIONAL FOOD FROM WALES
A Hippocrene Original Cookbook
Bobby Freeman
Welsh food and customs through the centuries. This book combines over 260 authentic, proven recipes with cultural and social history.
332 pages • 5 1/2 x 8 1/2 • 0-7818-0527-9 • NA $24.95 • (638)

TRADITIONAL FOOD FROM SCOTLAND: THE EDINBURGH BOOK OF PLAIN COOKERY RECIPES
A delightful assortment of Scottish recipes and helpful hints for the home—this classic volume offers a window into another era.
336 pages • 5 1/2 x 8 • 0-7818-0514-7 • W • $11.95pb • (620)

TRADITIONAL RECIPES FROM OLD ENGLAND
Arranged by country, this charming classic features the favorite dishes and mealtime customs from across England, Scotland, Wales and Ireland.
128 pages • 5 x 8 1/2 • 0-7818-0489-2 •W • $9.95pb • (157)

THE ART OF IRISH COOKING
Monica Sheridan
Nearly 200 recipes for traditional Irish fare.
166 pages • 5 1/2 x 8 1/2 • 0-7818-0454-X • W • $12.95pb • (335)

All prices subject to change. **To purchase Hippocrene Books** contact your local bookstore, call (718) 454-2366, or write to: HIPPOCRENE BOOKS, 171 Madison Avenue, New York, NY 10016. Please enclose check or money order, adding $5.00 shipping (UPS) for the first book and $.50 for each additional book.

DATE			